S0-CFS-005

heraldry for the designer

WILLIAM METZIG

heraldry
for
the
designer

VNR **VAN NOSTRAND REINHOLD COMPANY**
NEW YORK CINCINNATI LONDON TORONTO MELBOURNE

In memory of the late Dr. Karl Friedrich Leonhardt, Director of Archives, City of Hannover, Germany, who introduced me to heraldry and taught me to love it as much as he did.

First published in paperback in 1983

Library of Congress Catalog Card Number 69-16376
ISBN 0-442-26358-9

All rights reserved. No part of this work may be reproduced or used in any form or by any means—graphic, electronic, or mechanical, including photocopying, recording, taping, or information storage and retrieval systems—without written permission of the publisher.

Printed in the United States of America

Van Nostrand Reinhold Company Inc.
135 West 50th Street
New York, New York 10020

Fleet Publishers
1410 Birchmount Road
Scarborough, Ontario M1P 2E7, Canada

Van Nostrand Reinhold
480 Latrobe Street
Melbourne, Victoria 3000, Australia

Van Nostrand Reinhold Company Limited
Molly Millars Lane
Wokingham, Berkshire, RG11 2PY England

Cloth edition published 1969 by Van Nostrand Reinhold Company Inc.

16   15   14   13   12   11   10   9   8   7   6   5   4   3   2   1

Contents

Preface

This book was not written to add to the vast scholarly literature that already exists in the field of heraldry; nor is it written as a "how-to" book. Rather it is a book written by a graphic artist who, as a young man, fell in love with heraldry and, fifty years later, is still fascinated by its design possibilities. As such, it outlines some of the basic elements of this rich source for creative graphics, for few will deny that heraldry, though born in the Middle Ages, retains its charm to the present day.

Accordingly, the book is directed to the modern designer, so that he too may recognize the immense design potential that heraldry affords when used in all its richness. For although we see it continuously used around us — from dog-food labels to prestigious car emblems — it is, for the most part, ill-used, and its effectiveness is diminished thereby.

It is commonly known that heraldry was developed as a "language" used to visually communicate not only a bearer's identity, but many other facts about him. And because it was a symbol-language, precise "rules" had to be established for universal comprehension. But what is seldom realized is that it was these very parameters that fostered the inventive genius of the heraldic designers, who were challenged then by the same artistic problems that designers face today: to visually convey facts and impressions, with given restrictions, in a limited space. The accomplishments of the heraldic designers were so outstanding that more than five hundred years later we can still apply their creative ideas to modern graphic problems.

I have tried, in the pages that follow, to provide the designer with an orientation to heraldic design. And, to facilitate an understanding of this basic material, I have omitted from the text those impediments of detail characteristically found in books on heraldry. For instance, rather than cluttering the format with captions, I placed all the blazoning in a section at the back of the book, where it is keyed to the illustration numbers. For the sake of consistency, the captions of those illustrations not requiring blazonry, as well as credits applicable to certain illustrations, have also been integrated into this section.

Similarly, tangential rules and explanations of certain heraldic aspects are treated separately as appendices in order not to interrupt continuity. Of course, any nomenclature and terminology germane to understanding are incorporated in the text. A glossary-index is provided as an additional reference.

In principle, I have adhered to the rigors of heraldic design "rules" because they are necessary to make such design effective. The rules, however, are not as confining as they might appear; there is much leeway left for creative imagination to blossom — for what is presented here should only plant a seed.

More than 5000 years ago

More than 5,000 years ago, at the dawn of Western civilization, Egyptian and Assyrian kings and priests chose lions, eagles, and imaginary beasts as symbols of their gods, their fears, their fantasies, and their power. They personified these symbols with all that was human, and much that was superhuman. And in this glorification artists and craftsman created innumerable monuments, buildings, reliefs, and pottery of such admirable styling and conception that their work was to influence the civilized world for centuries to come. Arresting and fascinating, their simplifications of men and beasts remain masterpieces of artistic imagination.

Once this style of ornamental linear richness reached its peak, it flowered unabated and unchanged for over four hundred years. After that, however, the creative force in Egypt lost much of its originality and sank into the quicksand of routine and redundancy, eventually to be overshadowed by the sublimely mature art of the enlightened Greeks across the Mediterranean.

Yet, centuries later, the devices and symbols created for heraldic designs were strikingly similar to the art and symbolism of these earlier cultures. The link between the two is perhaps coincidence. Certainly, the purposes of heraldic symbolism and those of ancient art differed sharply: the former was a codified system of genealogical identification, while the latter served as representations of deities.

One explanation for the similarity might lie in the natural consistency with which artists through the ages saw the inherent characteristics of the symbols they used. For example, the lion has always been regarded as an intrepid and powerful animal. As early as 3000 B.C. a courageous-looking lion, symbolizing a victorious king, is found on a slate palette depicting a battlefield of corpses and carrion vultures. In the fourth century B.C. the famous Lion of Chaeronea was the symbol chosen for a battle monument erected by Philip of Macedonia to honor his valiant dead. A rampant lion, the dauntless symbol of St. Mark, appears in a book of gospels used in spreading Christianity among Europe's barbarian tribes in the seventh century A.D. Five hundred years later, this lion, appearing as a badge of the powerful Norman kings, was to become one of the earliest known heraldic charges, and eventually the symbol that dominated English heraldry.

7

6

Similarly, the eagle, chosen by heraldic designers as a symbol of power and might, can also be traced to antiquity. In Figure 6 we see the god Ningirsu holding an eagle as his emblem. This ancient representation of the Sumerian god of war was done in 3000 B.C., yet the eagle he holds has a stylization and ornamentation extraordinarily similar to those that appeared in countless coats of arms throughout medieval Europe.

The god Ashur, appearing on a bas-relief (Fig. 7) dated about 1000 B.C., was a fanciful creature with an eagle's head and wings, who played a prominent role in the Assyrian version of the Babylonian legend of creation. Such deities were venerated as symbols of might, guarding against the forces of real and imaginary adversaries.

But, some nine hundred years later, these and other peoples who looked to their eagle-like gods to protect them would fall before the silver eagles leading the invincible legions of Rome in forging an empire of their conquests. "Of all the birds with which we are acquainted," said Pliny the Elder, "the eagle is the most noble and the most remarkable for its strength." Thus, mounted on standards (Fig. 8) raised high over phalanxes, the eagle became the emblem of Imperial Rome and a symbol of its might.

It is not surprising, therefore, that the early heraldic designers adopted this symbol for the very same reasons that it was venerated by former cultures. The eagle dominated the armory of continental Europe for centuries thereafter.

Similar parallels also existed in the functional uses of ornamental devices. For instance, Sekhmet, goddess of war, is shown in Figure 9 wearing a pair of bull's horns and ornamented eagle feathers over her lion head — devices, no doubt, meant to frighten the enemy in battle. Surely intimidation was also intended by the ornamented crests worn by armored knights as they vied in combat or fought in battle. The functions of both are rooted in the same psychology of warfare: a frightened opponent is a demoralized one. Incidentally, Sekhmet, a minor Egyptian deity, was part woman, part lioness, a kind of invention characteristic of many later heraldic monsters.

8

7

There may be yet another, very practical reason for some of the amazing similarities between heraldic charges and ancient symbols and forms. Though their purposes differed, both ancient and medieval artists employed a "picture language," which necessitated creating pictorial symbolizations of the subject matter being conveyed. Later linguistic refinements often changed the meanings of the symbols they created, but their graphic appearance remained consistent: pictorially, a tree continued to look like a tree even though its meaning or symbolism was no longer the same. Perhaps, then, it was the heraldic designer's need to express his ideas in word-signs that accounts for the reappearance of ancient symbols and forms in armorial bearings hundreds of years later.

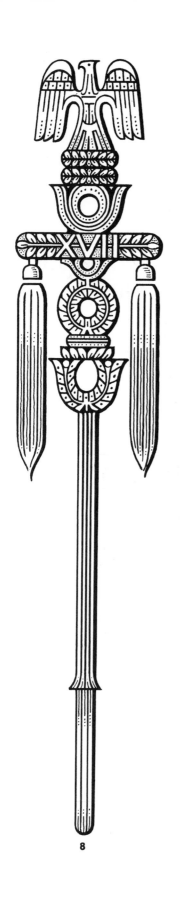

8

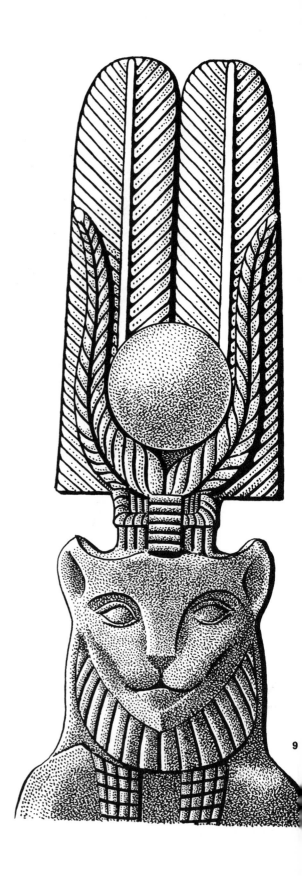

9

10

The Egyptian bas-relief below provides an example: each of the lines and symbols appearing on this 2700 B.C. rebus reappeared as heraldic charges to express much the same thoughts. The cross, for instance, was used as a sign of divinity in both pagan and Christian cultures; the wavy lines were depictions of water; and the droplet form, a representation of blood or tears. Thus, these and other forms and symbols have been similarly created and re-created over and over again by culture after culture since time began, for this phenomenon is the way of human experience.

And finally, if we were to test the coincidence of precedence even further, we would find a similarity not only in the elements of heraldic arms, but in the form itself. Look closely at the Assyrian amulet of a scarab above; it is almost a perfect coat of arms, with shield, crest, and mantle.

Indeed, the assertion that the art of heraldry is rooted in antiquity can be made convincingly. Surely, the symbols and forms that constituted armorial insignia parallel those of prior cultures; the links connecting them are unmistakable. Nonetheless, heraldic art cannot be considered merely an historical development of ancient art, because heraldry is a concept that did not evolve — it happened!

11

Enter Heraldry

Sometime during the earlier generations of the twelfth century, what might be termed an "identity explosion" occurred; because of it, the concept of heraldry originated. It was a practical innovation, born of the necessity to establish signs of personal identity. Devices of identity did exist before this time, but they were primarily seals used to identify bearers as being under the aegis of particular kings and popes; as such, they were not personal to the bearer.

The innovation heraldry introduced was the creation of an ingenious system that codified insignia of personal identification, thereby establishing an exclusiveness of armorial bearings, a uniformity of nomenclature, a universality of cognizance, and, most important, a perpetuity through heritage. It is this system that distinguishes heraldry and severs it conceptually from all links to the past.

Exactly what caused the urgency for personal identity prompting heraldry is, of course, a matter of conjecture. In all probability a number of circumstances contributed to it. By the beginning of the twelfth century, feudal knights, smitten with wanderlust by the tales of the first Crusaders, began to travel, searching here and there, alone and in bands, to practice the only trade they knew: combat. However, the combatants often found difficulty in determining who their opponents were, if indeed they were opponents, since their mode of defensive armor was such that it made them virtually indistinguishable from one another. This handicap was, in effect, the first "packaging problem" — the identification of a hidden content. The solution was to adopt easily recognizable and individualistic signs with which the shields and garments of the knights could be decorated as a means of identification. Thus, individual combat and battles of opposing factions provide a need for identification, and no doubt gave impetus to the use of personal insignia.

But, historically, the facts belie this cause as the major one, for such personal signs sprang up almost simultaneously all over Europe, and in any case it is hardly conceivable that rival knights would stop to parlay on such matters before they cut each other to pieces. Another vehicle then, must principally account for the rapid spread of the system called heraldry, and most likely it was the tournament — the most popular war game of the age.

Tournaments, with all their pomp and pageantry, were the order of the day at every major court of the land. They were taken just as seriously as actual warfare; a knight's reputation rose or fell on how he fared at such contests.

In order to enroll as a participant, a knight had to present his colors — or more precisely, his personal insignia — to the "major-domo" of the tournament: the court *herald*, who, among his other duties, was in charge of the proclamation and conduct of such affairs. Heralds thus became acknowledged authorities on the meanings and genealogies of armorial bearings and, by interchanging their knowledge, established the framework of what is appropriately called *heraldry*.

At tournaments, heralds took the role of "announcers." Their tasks were to marshall combats and announce challenges. The announcement, a short verbal description of insignia, was termed *blazonry* — from the German "blasen": to blow — because the herald used a trumpet to get the attention of the audience. (Blazonry, and its prescribed sequence, are described in Appendix G.)

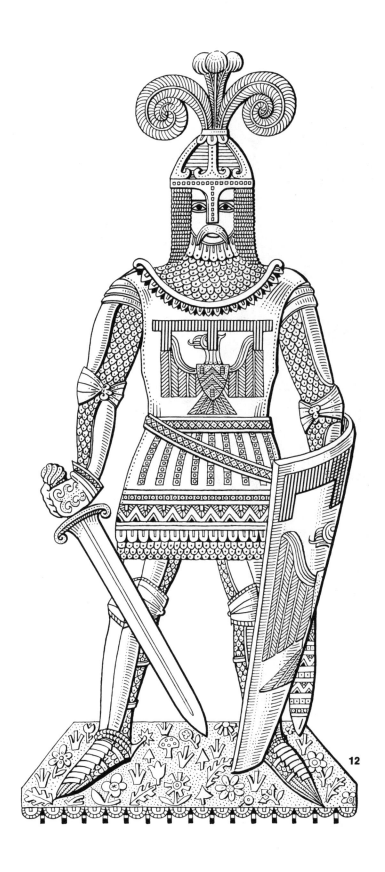

12

13

Tournaments were also the spawning ground for the proliferation of armory. Knights who were victorious in combat contests were often asked to join their host's court to defend his realm, or to exploit those of weaker neighbors. When these wars ended victoriously, the knights were often rewarded with parts of the conquered lands. And so new courts were born, and new heraldic devices had to be redesigned. Following the feudal customs, the new lords were no less eager for conquests — some chose war, some marriage. So eventually the realms, formerly of a few rulers, became, through generations, divided into many smaller courts, bringing about an unprecedented flourishing of heraldic art.

In the beginning only the lords and their knights carried the new devices. Later all the followers, the yeomen and the knaves-in-arms, adopted their lord's heraldic symbols and displayed them on their shields and battle dress. Sometimes they used them as pennants on their lances, as rallying points in battle. In this manner standards and flags were born, and likewise the military insignia of today. It is also safe to assume that the colorful outfits of these early fighting forces were the beginnings of the military uniform.

Heraldry made its major contribution in the field of design. The striking power of heraldic art is due, in part, to the limitation of space and color, which necessitated severe simplicity of form and content. The present-day designer is confronted with these same conditions when he has to create a trademark, a textile pattern, a package, or a label. The symbols of heraldry are an almost inexhaustible source of design ideas, for, in more than one way, the corporate identity is the heraldry of today.

Elements of a Coat of Arms

Crest
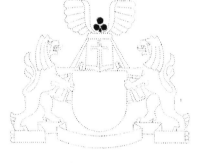

Torse

Badge
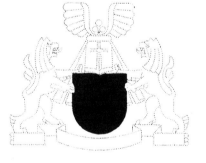

Helmet
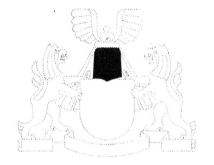

Shield
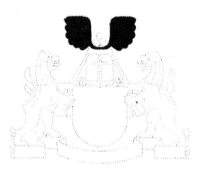

Mantling

Supporters

Scroll & Motto

15

16

The *shield*, or *escutcheon*, is the most important element of a coat of arms because it displays the *charges* that constitute the insignia of the bearer. In fact, an escutcheon is frequently used without other elements as a *shield of arms*, as, for example, on the so-called *Rolls of Arms*, a kind of registry for armorial insignia. Figure 18 shows such a Roll as background to a mounted knight in full armor.

The area within a shield is called a *field*, and its surface is divided into parts given specific names used in referring to (or blazoning) the location of charges. For instance, the upper third of the field is called the *chief*; the lower third, the *base.* (The nomenclature of other parts can be found in Appendix B.) With respect to location, two terms that often cause confusion should be clarified: the left and right sides of the shield are always labeled from the wearer's view: his right side is called *dexter;* his left, *sinister.*

Throughout the history of armory, shields have assumed various shapes, ranging from the rudimentary flatiron shape of Gothic heraldry to those more intricate forms so characteristic of the Romantic movement. Some of the basic shield forms are shown opposite.

The charges that adorn the fields are the essence of heraldic design. Actually, the term "charge" encompasses all the figures, symbols, or devices used in, or on, any element of the coat of arms. The early designers and craftsmen incorporated all things imaginable in their work, from nature's creations of earth and sky to man-made monsters. The stars, the sun, the moon, lightning and thunder, trees and plants, and all animate and inanimate things were used in a marvelous panorama of form and color.

There are, of course, countless classical charges, of which only a few can be shown in this book. Yet, for the designer, this sampling should more than suggest the applicability of heraldic charges to modern design problems. For in the myriad of ordinaries, lions, eagles, flowers, and even monsters, he will find a treasure trove of forms that can yield fascinating trademarks or, perhaps, interesting package designs. And, if he muses a bit, he may discover new and contemporary expressions of bygone motifs that can be adapted to a wide range of design needs with amazing suitability.

The *helmet* appears above the shield roughly in the position where the bearer's head would be. Helmets were usually depicted as being made of iron or steel; those of gold were reserved for bearers of noble or royal birth.

The styling of a helmet generally corresponds to the period it represents. For example, Renaissance and baroque types were considerably more elaborate than were the pot helms worn during the early times of chain mail. The latter is the simplest form of all the various types, and I have used it almost exclusively in this book.

For some heraldic purposes the type and positioning of the helmet has special significance. For example, in English heraldry, the type of helmet used served as an additional indication of rank. Meaning was also attached to whether the helmet was shown *en face* (i.e., straight on) or in dexter or sinister profile. But these are no longer considerations in modern heraldry.

An important factor in fashioning a helmet is to design it in correct proportion to the shield. (Appendix A contains proportioning guidelines.) Style is another design aspect that should be carefully considered. Early helmet designs tended to be authentic representations even to the extent of showing rivets and hinges in detail. Over the years, however, stylistic changes caused the helmet to take on weird and improbable shapes, and, while such design abstractions are permissible, the helmet's realistic function should not be sacrificed. Also, from a realistic point of view it should be remembered that, theoretically, the perspiring wearer should be able first to get his head into it, and then survive inside it; in other words, the neck must not be too narrow.

The *mantle* was a falling cloth garment worn over helmet and armor to protect the knight from the heat of the sun and his armor from the elements. Secured by the torse to the base of the crest, the mantle displays two colors, usually the principal color and the metal tincture of the shield, and is so arranged that the metal tincture is shown as the cloak's inside lining, while the color appears on its outside. Primarily for artistic purposes, early heraldic designers usually slit and turned the mantle so that the parts showing hue and metal were in approximately equal amounts. Similarly, modern designers can slit, turn, twist, or fold the mantle to their heart's content, just as long as the exposed parts of color and metal cover approximately the same amount of area. It is here, in the shaping of the mantle, that the designer finds complete freedom. There are no restrictions, except that the mantle be recognizable as such.

17

The *crest* is a decoration attached to the top of the helmet, generally repeating either the main charge of the shield, or a variation of it. Originally a painted piece of wood or leather, the crest was also used to depict an additional feat or accomplishment of the bearer. By and large, crests were devices like horns, eagle's wings, lions, or monsters, although literally countless other objects were also used. Some unusual ones are shown above.

The *torse*, sometimes called a *wreath* or a *twist*, attaches the mantle to the crest by twisting two ends of the mantle around the base of the crest. The twisting accounts for the alternating colors in the torse, usually shown in six parts, beginning with the color of the metal, which then alternates with the principal color. The torse originally served to hide the method used to attach the crest to the helm.

20

The *badge* was in many cases a predecessor to a coat of arms as a sign of personal identity and, as such, it is not considered an integral part of armorial bearings. However, when incorporated, badges were considered charges and, conversely, charges in the shield were developed into badges where none had existed previously.

As a matter of history, an important and brutal struggle for England's monarchy is identified by a badge. This famous fratricide saw John, Duke of Lancaster, whose badge was the red rose, pitted against Edmund, Duke of York, the white rose, in a long and bitter contest — and the name "War of the Roses" entered the annals of English history.

Another famous badge (bottom, left), the "Sun in its Splendor," chosen by Edward IV, was immortalized by Shakespeare's lines in *Richard III*: "Now is the winter of our discontent/ Made glorious summer by this sun of York."

Because the badge was more a symbol of identification than of rank, it gained wide application. Often it served as a decorative emblem on property and household goods. Eventually, vassals adopted their lord's badge and wore it as their own. Later, countries, cities, guilds, and other kinds of organized bodies used badges as part of their insignia, seals, and flags. Today badges are used as military insignia and other official and quasi-official emblems.

Supporters appear on either side of the shield as guardians of the arms. They were often representations of human, and sometimes divine, beings. Usually they were real or imaginary animals and creatures, sometimes menacing, armed with teeth or weapons.

Although supporters are sometimes used as a decorative element in commercial design, they really should be reserved for arms of titled families or for those bearing authority, like governments and institutions.

The *scroll* was usually fashioned as a ribbon from the ground the supporters stood on. Generally a *motto* was inscribed on it. Mostly written in Latin, mottoes were maxims expressing a "leitmotif" or admonition. Unlike the insignia, mottoes were not exclusive, and often lasted only a generation.

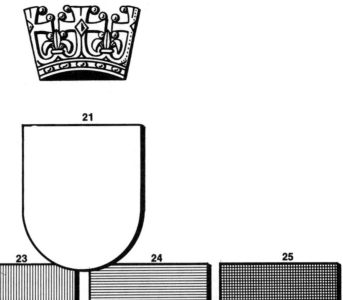

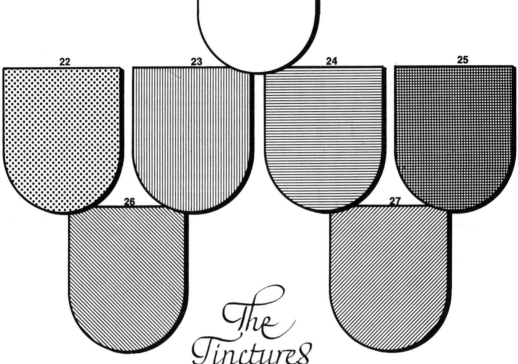

The Tinctures

Basic to all coats of arms is *tincture*. Tincture is the term used for the colors, metals, and furs used in heraldry. In practice, the metals, gold and silver, are grouped with five selected hues to make up the seven "colors" to which heraldic design is limited. There is, however, no restriction in using shades of these colors. Each tincture has a specific name handed down from medieval times: *or* (gold) is yellow; *argent* (silver), white; *gules*, red; *azure*, blue; *vert*, green; *sable*, black; and *purpure*, purple. Also from medieval times comes the very important general rule concerning their application: color (i.e., hue) must not be placed upon color, nor metal upon metal. A red field, for example, can only be adorned with a metal tincture, and vice versa.

In addition to being decorative, color was highly functional in the language of heraldry. Purple, for example, denoted high rank, church, or royalty. Color was also a method of *differencing*, as, for example, a red lion from a gold lion. In heraldic publications, however, black was frequently the only color available; it therefore became necessary to find a way to represent the colors while only using black. Such a way was found at the end of the sixteenth century, when a system of tincture using lines and dots

was devised. The practice was adopted by printers and engravers and eventually became universally accepted. Although tinctures are still used to depict colors in modern coats of arms, this practice is rarely found in commercial applications of heraldry.

The top shield (above, left) represents the tincture silver. The others are, from left to right, gold, red, blue, black, green, and purple.

Besides the seven colors, tinctures also include vair and ermine furs. Vairs were originally furs taken from the bellies of small animals, probably squirrels, and used as linings for medieval garments. As tinctures, they were usually stylized in various patterns of blue on white. It is permissible, but rare, to use other colors.

The *ermine* fur (Fig. 28, above) is represented by the same kind of ermine tail-ends used to decorate royal mantles. When reversed (i.e., white tails on black) the fur was called *ermines* (Fig. 29). Not shown above are *erminois* (black tails on gold) and *pean* (gold tails on black). The other furs above are *vairs* (Figs. 30, 31), followed by *countervair*, and, on the bottom row, *vair en point counterpotent,* and *potent.*

23

LINES

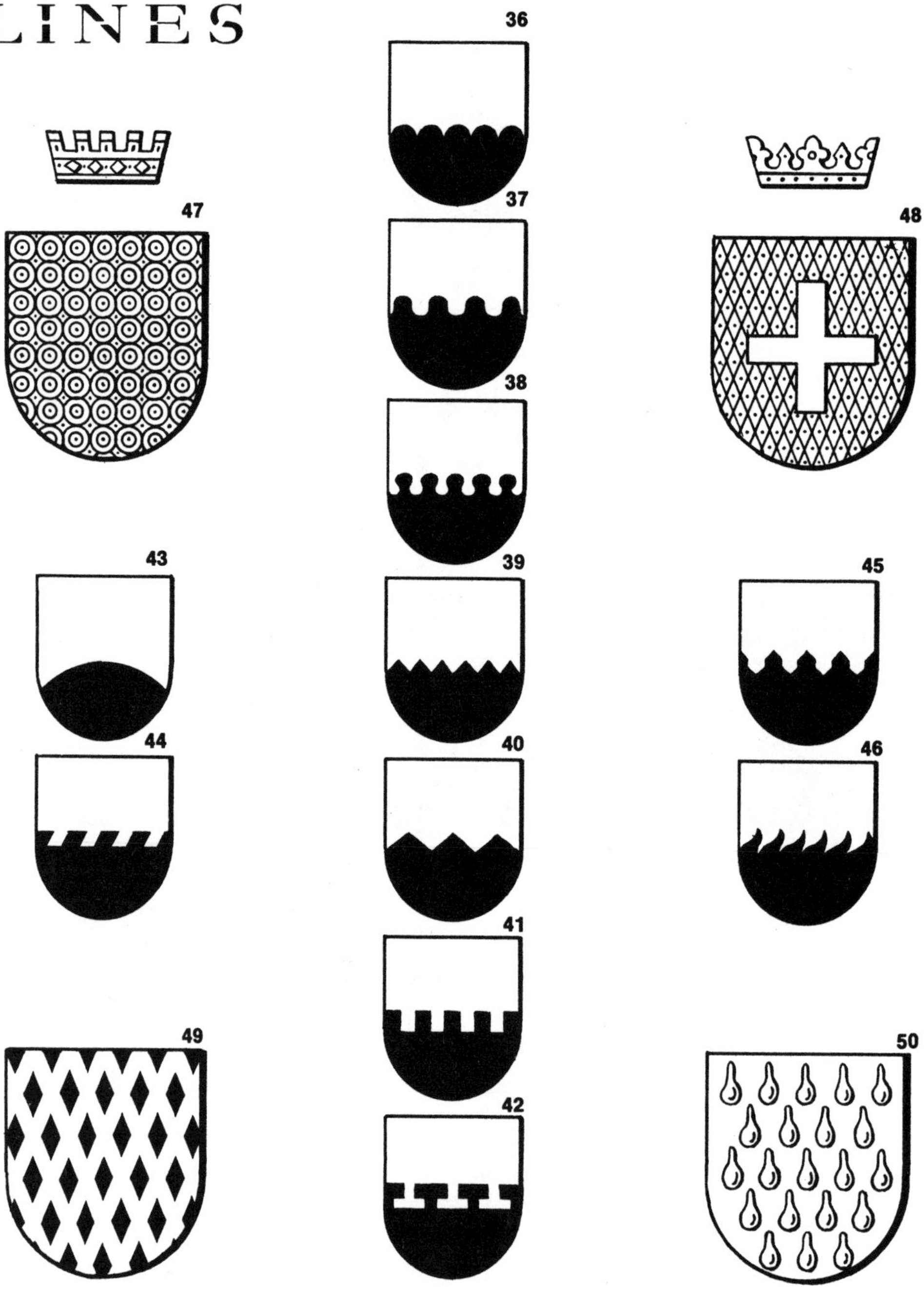

The earliest, and most common, form of heraldic design partitioned the shield into two or more parts by devices called *lines*, both plain and ornamental. Lines have specific names, frequently descriptive of their form. For instance, *wavy*, in Figure 37, suggests waves, and *embattled* (Fig. 41) depicts the configuration on castle walls. The meaning of some terms, however, is less obvious. For example, *potenty* (Fig. 42) is a term probably devised as a pictorial representation of the Chaucerian word for "crutches."

Above, identified in numerical sequence, are some basic lines: *invected*, *wavy*, *nebuly*, *indented*, *dancetty*, *embattled*, *potenty*, *arched*, *raguly*, *urdy*, and *radiant*. Although shown here horizontally, lines can, of course, run in any direction.

Other lines, forming repeat patterns, were often used to make plain fields more ornamental; examples are the techniques of *diapering* (Figs. 47, 48), *fusily* (Fig. 49), and *goutté* (Fig. 50). These patterns offer a rich cache for textile design.

Fields and Ordinaries

The use of partitioning lines made possible a broad range of design variation for heraldic arms. Basically, dividing any field into two, three, or four parts is termed *party* (i.e., parted). Such divisions, made in vertical, horizontal, and diagonal directions, form separately, or in combination, the basic partitions of the field, called *party per*: *fess* (Fig. 52), *pale* (Fig. 53), *bend sinister* (Fig. 55), *chevron* (Fig. 56), *saltire* (Fig. 57), and *cross* (Fig. 58). This nomenclature of direction permeates the language of heraldry and is the backbone of blazonry.

In addition to simple parting, fields were also varied by further subdivision. For instance, the addition of an *odd* number of bands dividing a field into an *even* number of parts created patterns that had special names, viz.: *barry* (Fig. 60), *paly* (Fig. 64), *bendy* (Fig. 61), and *chevronny* (Fig. 63). Only the name *barry*, derived from *bar*, in this case a term replacing *fess*, is not derived from the nomenclature of party. To achieve further variation, lines of partition were also made ornamental, as for example, *bendy dancetty* (Fig. 62) and *paly wavy* (Fig. 66). And for greater design complexity, partitions were combined, as in *per pale and barry* (Fig. 59), and *checky* (Fig. 68) — a special name used for the combination of *paly* and *barry*. Thus, simple and complex partied and varied fields provided the ground on which ordinaries and other charges were placed.

The *ordinaries* are the most "ordinary" charge used in heraldic design, and probably the oldest method of bearer distinction. In the beginning, ordinaries were formed by merely coloring the strips of wood or metal used as reinforcements to strengthen the shield; this practice soon led to painting bands of colors even where there were no reinforcing strips. Eventually, from the various combinations of vertical, horizontal, or diagonal bands, simple designs of contrasting colors were created. Unfortunately the labels adopted to identify these ordinaries were borrowed from the terminology used in the nomenclature of fields and, therefore, tend at first to be confusing. For example, a vertical band is an ordinary called a *pale* (Fig. 72). Other ordinaries are called: *fess* (Fig. 69), *bend* (Figs. 76, 100), *chevron* (Fig. 78), *saltire* (Fig. 87), and *cross* (Fig. 89). *Chief* (Fig. 51), *pile* (Fig. 77), and *pall* (Fig. 80) are also ordinaries.

Although the terms used to identify ordinaries were standard, the fashioning of the forms themselves was left to the discretion of the medieval designer and, as a result, there still is no firm agreement among armorists as to the band width of ordinaries. Many of the variations in width emerged as distinct ordinaries; in most cases, however, their origins as diminutives of original forms are indicated by their derivative names. For instance, *chevronnels* (Figs. 81, 86) are diminutives of chevrons. In the same manner a *pallet* would be a narrower pale, and a *bendlet* a narrower bend. Two exceptions are *bar* (Fig. 71), considered the diminutive of a fess, and *shakefork* (Fig. 84), diminutive of a pall. Terms of further diminution also obscure their origins. For instance, a fess or a bend flanked by very thin barlike lines is said to be *cotised*, as in Figures 70 and 79. However these same lines flanking a pale (Fig. 73) cause it to be *endorsed*.

The proper width of diminutive ordinaries is, as in the case of the ordinaries themselves, a matter of interpretation rather than rule. For this reason guidelines for the proportioning of ordinaries are prescribed in Appendix C.

The simple ordinary was frequently the predominant, and often the sole, charge on the shields of early armory. However, even with all the combinations available, the number of variations possible never seemed sufficient, and time after time the inventiveness of heraldic designers was tested anew. Invariably they rose to the challenge by ingeniously devising new and exciting forms. For instance, compounded forms were created by combining more than one ordinary on a single field, as in Figures 65 and 67. Yet it remained for concepts like *counterchange* to make possible a raft of new

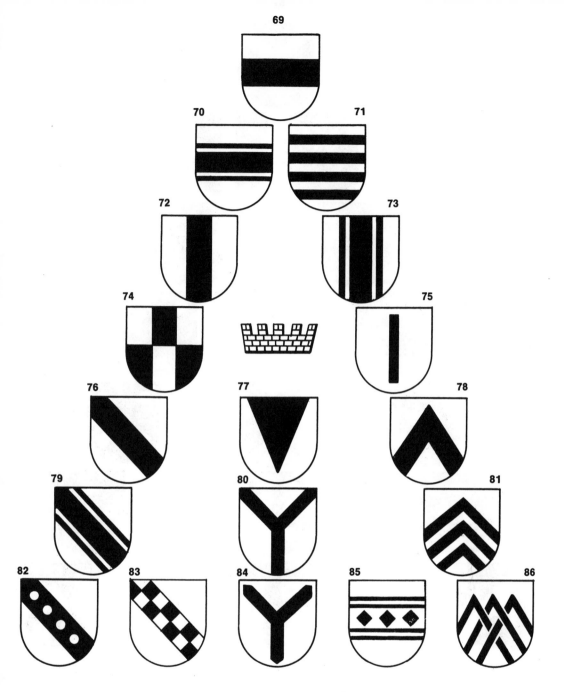

ordinaries. The mosaic patterns formed by counterchange result from exchanging the color of a part of an ordinary with the color of the field (as in Figures 74 and 102).

Another innovation that produced almost infinite possibilities of variation was the introduction of additional charges placed on the bands of ordinaries. For example, the bend (Fig. 82), saltire (Fig. 88), and party pale (Fig. 98) are charged with roundels. Roundels, as well as other charges, are commonly used (in lieu of bands) as ordinaries. Those shown here are in: *chief*, *fess*, *pale*, *bend*, *chevron*, *saltire*, *pile*, and *cross*.

As the evolution of the ordinaries became more sophisticated, a large group of secondary forms was classified as *subordinaries*. Characteristically, they were smaller and less dominating, but no less definite in form than other ordinaries.

27

The *bordure* (Fig. 103), for example, may have been invented for differencing purposes, but was later used exclusively as a subordinary. Similarly, an *inescutcheon* (Fig. 104), a smaller shield differently tinctured within the main shield, was a device used to illustrate a special feat or accomplishment of the bearer.

A border outlined within a shield forming an inner shield is called an *orle* (Fig. 105). It may appear in line or be fashioned from small charges. Figure 107, for example, would be an *orle of roundels*. A double orle is called a *tressure* (Fig. 106). Sometimes a *canton* (Fig. 118) is placed over both of them to carry charges of different devices. A canton cut diagonally in half into a pennant-like shape is termed a *gyron* (Fig. 117). It, too, can contain charges, as can the two vertical curves called *flanches* (Fig. 116).

A *lozenge* (Fig. 108) is a diamond form, and a *fusil* (Fig. 109) a slimmer diamond form. Also, a lozenge within a lozenge created the *mascle* (Fig. 110), while a roundel in the center of a lozenge made it a *rustre* (Fig. 111). The mascle, when interlaced with a bendlet and a bendlet sinister, became a *fret* (Fig. 114). And *fretty* (Fig. 112), naturally,

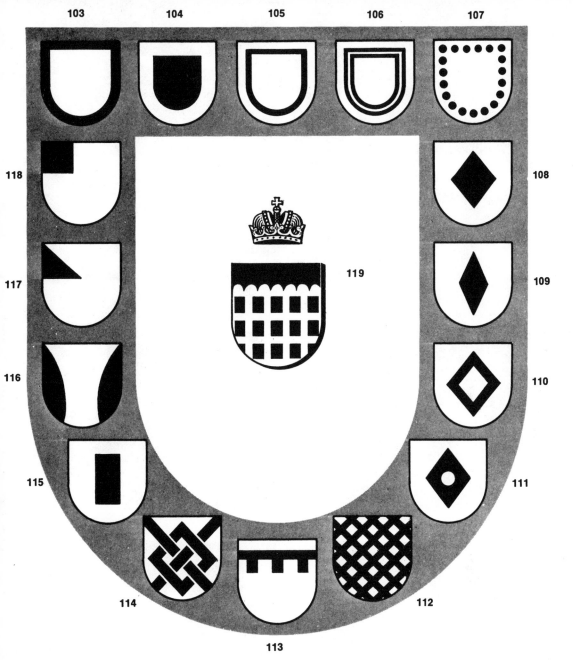

is a field covered with frets. Similarly, *billety* (Fig. 119) is a field of billets. The *billet* (Fig. 115) is a rectangular form thought to represent the shape of a brick; more likely, it was derived from the French "billet" (letter).

All these forms were popular charges widely used ornamentally. The *label* (Fig. 113), however, had additional significance; as the symbol of cadency, it signifies the oldest son. (This and other marks of cadency are explained in Appendix E).

There are other subordinaries and many other ordinaries that have been formed and formulated since the early twelfth century; in all they constitute an incredible body of design ideas. Yet in devising these inventions armorists also generated a plethora of terms that, unfortunately, has intimidated many of those who might have otherwise ventured further into the subject. This, however, need not be the case. Surely, to learn the language of heraldry takes a little effort, but upon closer inspection a marvelous logic can be found in its construction, and this fascinating discovery will make the effort worthwhile.

The *cross* is an ordinary — perhaps the most renowned. Appealing in its simplicity and decorativeness, the cross has appeared in various forms and on countless shields, especially on those of earlier design. In all likelihood, its proliferation as a symbol is due primarily to its religious significance. Religion in the Middle Ages played a dominant role in the lives of kings and knaves; it was a living part of the feudal culture. Hence, the sign of the cross permeates medieval heraldry, and its use gave rise to an incredible number of variations. Above are some of the better known crosses, among them: the *partriarchal* cross (Fig. 122), of ecclesiastical heraldry; *Jerusalem* crosses (opposite, and Fig. 127 above), used in the Crusades, and the *maltese* cross (Fig. 134), made famous by the Templars. The plain cross is shown *couped* (Fig. 121), *voided* (Fig. 123), *quarter-pierced — fimbriated* (Fig. 124), and *pointed* (Fig. 131). Some of the ornamental crosses shown are *moline* (Fig. 128), *fourché* (Fig. 129), *cercelé* (Fig. 130), and *floretty* (Fig. 135).

The Charges

LIONS

The *lion*, which dominated Norman and English heraldry, was chosen for the symbolism of its strength and awesome beauty. It was regarded as king of its realm, "the high and the mighty."

Early heraldic lions were more ornamentally drawn than the rather naturalistic forms of the late Middle Ages. These early lions, shown mostly in aggressive attitudes, were real masterpieces of design expressing all the beast's ferocity and majesty.

In later representations, the lion was shown tamed and dignified, reduced almost to a domestic animal: sitting, pacing, sleeping, and sometimes even with its tail between its legs. Nonetheless, in any pose, the lion remains a beast of beauty and grace.

Because of the countless uses of the lion as a symbol, the proud bearers of this kingly charge had to find ways of differencing, and so a variety of "poses" were invented and standardized to differentiate the charges.

Thus, specific terms were introduced into the language of heraldry to identify precisely the more than one hundred combinations resulting from various predetermined positions of the lion's body, paws, head, and tail. These terms used, with few exceptions, in the blazoning of all animals and monsters, are explained and illustrated in Appendix D.

Often, however, only parts of a lion (or other creature) were used, and additional blazoning had to be devised. Figure 137, for example, is a lion's head *affronté*, which means that it is facing front.

A head in profile, couped at the neck, is shown in Figure 162. *Couped* means that the cut is made straight; cuts that are ragged, as if ripped off, are termed *erased* (Fig. 149). A lion cut off at the middle of its body is a *demi-lion* (Fig. 157). Sometimes a *paw* (Figs. 141, 142), or even a *tail* (Fig. 154), was used alone, but seldom as a main charge. Thus, endless variations, and sometimes oddities, were found to symbolize the virtues, real or imagined, of the bearer.

The lions on these pages are rendered in their classic stances and, for the most part, are contemporary treatments of the traditional Gothic lion.

153

154

155

162

156 **157** **158** **159**

160

161

163

164

165

166

167

168

169

170

171

172

173

174

Other Animals

Other animals also became heraldic charges. Prominent among them are the horse and the deer, but, of course, other beasts were not excluded.

Heraldic designers selected animals for their symbolism, which was usually based on a principal characteristic observed in, or attributed to, the creature. For instance, the *fox*, depicted in Figure 171, was noted for its cunning. The *steer* (Fig. 172), no doubt then, as now, considered a commodity, probably represented possession of a herd.

A common charge was the head of a *boar* (Fig. 173) usually shown couped or erased. The boar was a vicious animal with razor-sharp tusks. It took courage and skill to hunt and kill one, and its vanquished head served well as a badge of accomplishment. As for the *elephant*, it had a number of connotations. It was huge and mighty — attributes most knights coveted. To many it must have represented the legendary lands of the East. And even today its purported memory is envied by us all.

Figure 175 is a *bear collared*, *muzzled*, and *chained* — a condition signifying to its ferocity. Also a common charge, it probably suggested the cruel sport of bear-baiting practiced in the Middle Ages. The *camel*, long known as the "ship of the desert," was a symbol brought back from the arid wastelands of Africa, and might have symbolized endurance. The savage *wolf's head* recalls the resourceful predator that struck terror into countless hearts.

Figure 178 is a *wildcat*, a feline relative of the lion; though just as ferocious, it lacks the lion's regal symbolism. The *ram*, of course, is a stubborn, cantankerous force that no one dares get in the way of — characteristics true of many ambitious knights.

184

185

186

Seals are always fun and make great design elements, but they were totally unknown in classical heraldry; so were *kangaroos*, before the eighteenth century. Both are representative of modern heraldic charges. Finally, the *porcupine*, with its "armor" bristling like the *mace* in dexter chief, is an appropriate symbol of the medieval warrior.

Members of the *deer* family were very important in heraldic design. The deer itself came closer to being regarded as a "sacred" creature than any other animal. For one thing, unlike lions, deer were familiar and plentiful. Roaming the hills and forests throughout Europe, they epitomized grace and elegance. Huntsmen stalked them, kings protected them, and heraldic designers immortalized them.

187

The *horse*, on the other hand, was so important that the entire age of knighthood reflects its name, for chivalry is derived from the old French word *chevalerie*, meaning "horse soldiery." It was not uncommon for a horse's well-being to be placed before that of any household member. A warrior was often only as good as his horse, and feudal knights therefore cared well for their mounts.

They also honored horses in many heraldic charges, and in some cases, being the soldiers they were, they could not resist exaggerating a bit. Take the centerpiece above, for example. No matter how fast this horse seemed to run, it could not possibly have had wings. Wings belonged to other species — the mighty eagle for one.

July 1953
20 CENTS

ART DIRECTOR
& STUDIO NEWS

METZIG

Eagles

The eagle, with its magnificent wingspread enabling flights of dazzling heights, has fascinated man since the earliest times. Apparently, heraldic designers were no less awed than their ancestors, for this powerful bird was so widely used in armorial bearings that its position and appearance had to be meticulously blazoned to avoid confusion.

In addition to the countless renditions of the eagle itself, countless more were fashioned from its parts. Hence, a proliferation of heads, talons, and wings was developed in an endless parade of charges. Wings, especially, were favorite devices for crests, particularly in Renaissance arms.

Eagles, because they are covered with intricately formed feathers, lend themselves to a multiplicity of graphic renderings that no unfeathered creature can match. For this reason they have always been popular among designers. In the pages that follow are shown a number of the many, many stylizations possible.

190

The eagle on page 43 was done for the *Art Director and Studio News* years ago. It is a *preying* eagle handled in a decorative curlicue style. This kind of design is often overdone, with too many curlicues, or done incorrectly, with the curlicues not in the right direction. Both good and bad examples of this style can be found on old money bills, letterheads, and baroque lettering samples.

Figure 189 is an eagle *displayed* and *inverted*, as contrasted with Figure 190, in which it is *elevated* and *displayed*. Displayed wings are spread open; inverted indicates wingtips pointing downwards; elevated, pointing upwards. The two styles of execution are also in contrast. The former is a simplified treatment of the familiar bald eagle. The latter rendition is more severe, its density of lines suggesting the fluttering of wings. Since it has two heads, it is an Imperial Eagle, the sign of the Holy Roman Empire. Facing opposite directions, it symbolized sovereignty over East and West. Later, both the Austrian Emperor and the Russian Tsar adopted the double-headed eagle as their emblem.

ALTE FERT AQUILA

the birds

193

The rendition shown on page 46 is a form that is suggested when a lighter treatment is wanted, perhaps to be used on a colored background, or for blind embossing.

The eagle on page 47 is termed *impaled*, i.e., cut vertically in half. As a charge it could have been used to cover the dexter half of a shield. The other half could show any other charge, for instance a wife's coat of arms. In commercial graphics it may suggest poster art, or perhaps a book jacket.

The rendering in Figure 193 illustrates the use of a heavier technique to convey, in a stylized manner, the power and boldness of the bird. In Figure 194 a much airier technique is used, but the symbolism of strength is no less evident, particularly because the eagle is perched on a sword. The sword, however, is coupled with an olive sprig and, together with the lighter technique used, these elements suggest a readiness for war or peace.

The version shown in Figure 195 demonstrates that an eagle with wings unfolded can be presented in less height than the normally displayed eagle usually takes and yet not lose the powerful appearance of its form.

194

195

197

198

Above are two renditions of displayed eagles, both more contemporary, but still within the tradition of heraldic charges. And below them are so-called *alerion* eagles, that is, without beaks or legs.

Thus, the possible renditions of eagles are endless. Among the birds, its position in heraldry is as distinctive as the lion's among beasts, and it is indeed a creature worthy of the tribute.

The decorative forms of birds have always made them design favorites. On the wing, few species can rival them for beauty and grace. Alighted, they are models of extrava-

gant poise.

199

Other Birds

Perhaps the least pretentious bird used as an heraldic charge is the humble *martlet.* Often depicted without feet, and sometimes without legs — perhaps from the fact that they flew so fast that people believed they had no feet or legs — this small member of the European swallow family plays a distinctive role in heraldry: it is the mark of cadency for the fourth son. Beyond being a sign of differencing, the martlets, shown above, represent little in the way of symbolism, or even association; other birds, by and large, are stronger in this respect.

200

201

202

204

203

205

206

207

208

For instance, the *dove*, in Figure 200, has symbolized peace ever since Noah's time. Next to it are *swallows* in flight, an age-old sign of gracefulness. Then, the *swan*, an image of loveliness. The wise *owl*, a symbol of sagacity. The *ravens*, of scavenging, of darkness, croaking "nevermore." The *falcon*, bold, militant, and predatory. The *peacock* in its pride of beauty, mired in its vanity. The *rooster*, sign of morning or awakening, of virility shackled by conceit. The *ostrich*, of feathers, of lands down under, of heads buried in the sands, of apathy. All of them are alive with meanings suggested from the past and the present.

The *pelican* is another symbol that has been favored since the beginnings of heraldry. Invariably it was shown, as at right, *in its piety*, or *vulning itself* — a somewhat masochistic deed in which the pelican wounds its breast, drawing blood to feed its offspring. Bearers may have found this attitude appealing because it seemed noble and self-sacrificing; self-deception is apparently an age-old habit of man.

210

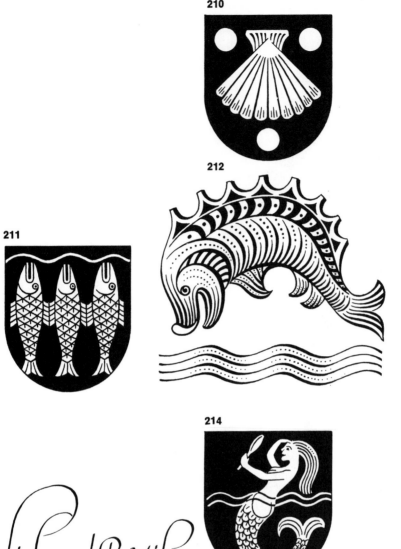

212

211

213

214

fish and Reptiles

The sea being so much a part of man's history, it is not surprising that fish have long been heraldic devices, though they fall among the less prominent charges.

The *dolphin* (Fig. 212 and p. 56) is a symbol dating back to the ninth century, when it was the emblem of the ancient Dauphiné region of France. From it came *dauphin*, the title given the eldest sons of the French kings, because they ruled there. The heraldic dolphin is always arched, i.e., *embowed*.

A familiar symbol from the sea is the scallop shell, known in heraldry as an *escallop*. It was worn by pilgrims to the Holy Land because it was the emblem of St. James, their patron saint. This symbolism, however, has not survived; today "sea shell" smacks of the sea and, incongruously, of a gasoline brand for which it is a trademark.

Heraldic treatment of fish did little to differentiate species, perhaps because to a non-angler most fish look pretty much alike. But the positions of the fish were considered important, and had special terms. Those in Figure 211 were blazoned *hauriant*, i.e., positioned vertically with heads rising upwards. Fish conversely shown are termed *urinant.* The other common position, swimming horizontally, is termed *naiant* (Fig. 213).

215

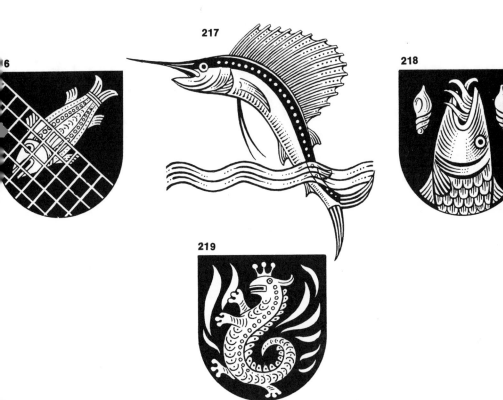

217

218

219

The mythical *mermaid* is firmly established as a marine symbol; heraldically, it is usually shown with comb and mirror.

The *sailfish* (center, above) is an exquisite form found in modern, rather than in classical, heraldry, because its natural habitat is the warm waters of the Atlantic Ocean bordering the New World. At its left is a *fish-in-net*, signifying, perhaps, a family of fishermen. At its right is a weird charge called a *barbel* (Fig. 218), which is the "feeler" attached to the mouth of a fish, used in its search for food.

Figure 215 is an heraldic *sea lion*, an imaginary creature bearing no resemblance to the one found in nature. This uninviting creature has the body of a lion and the tail of a fish. The *salamander* (Fig. 219), a gruesome companion, was a lizard-like creature generally surrounded by flames, and often fire-breathing. Actually reptilian, rather than marine, the salamander and the sea lion are sometimes classed as heraldic monsters.

220

221 222 223
224 225 226

Monsters

At the time heraldry flourished, man imagined the sea, the air, and the dark recesses below the ground to be inhabited by awesome mythical monsters. Odious creatures they were, some with scales and fiery breath, some half-lion and half-eagle, some winged beasts with snakes as tails, some wolves with eagle talons, and many other combinations of the possible and impossible.

People in those days believed in the existence of these creatures and greatly feared their might. Usually, the monsters were thought to be the guardians of treasures of gold and silver hidden in dark and impenetrable forests and caves. Or sometimes they were thought to be the evil captors of a fair maiden imprisoned in unapproachable ravines or atop inaccessible towers, pining for a knight to rescue her. (Of course, he did.)

And so he killed the dreaded dragon, or the odious cockatrice, or the terrible tyger, or the sinister wyvern. It is no wonder then, that when he was hailed for his symbolic victory over an imagined beast, he proudly displayed the vanquished monster in his coat of arms. And, as was the custom, his descendants continued to carry forward these invented creatures for hundreds of years.

228

Not all of these creatures, however, were horrible inventions; some were drawn from mythology. The *unicorn* (Fig. 224), for instance, was a popular animal in Greek and Roman mythology; it had the body of a horse, with a horn on its forehead, cloven hooves, a lion's tail, and a goatee. Artists of the Middle Ages frequently used it as a symbol of purity. In armory it often serves as a supporter (Fig. 13). Today the unicorn suggests things mythical or magic.

Another non-monster creature is *Pegasus* (Fig. 223), better known as the "flying horse," also of Greek mythology. A number of romantic legends as to how Pegasus became winged have been handed down, but generally people see in it a symbol of freedom and speed — an image that a large oil company effectively used as a trademark for many years.

The *cockatrice* (p. 58) perhaps takes the prize for hideousness among monsters: it had a cock's head, fiery wings, a horned, armored breast, powerful shanks with sharp talons, and a spiked snake's tail.

Running a close second in ugliness was the *opinicus* (Fig. 226), with its griffin's head and sharp beak, its lion's body, and its bear's tail (Fig. 231).

229

231

Possibly the most formidable monster was the *griffin* (Figs. 225, 230), with an eagle's upper body and a lion's hindquarters. It had a forked, horned beak and powerful claws. The *male griffin* (Fig. 229), though it had no wings, was covered with thorns. Either one was indeed a menacing enemy.

The fierce *wyvern* (Fig. 228) was probably the offspring of an errant dragon that mated with a cockatrice, for it is a composite of the two.

Another strange and frightening beast was the *tyger* (Fig. 222), basically a lion with a larger snout, more powerful legs, and spikes on its paws — a description probably arising from a gross misconception of what a real tiger looked like.

And finally, there is the old standby, the dragon (Fig. 221). This fire-breathing creature, with its grotesque dinosaurian head, forked tongue, batlike wings, sharp talons, and armor-scaled body, is perhaps the best known of all the nonexistent monsters. When St. George slew the dragon it became forever the fabric of countless legends.

Except perhaps for some bizarre applications, the modern designer may have difficulty in using these monsters for their symbolism. He should consider, however, the strong graphic forms they present, and not necessarily discard them out of hand.

Man has always been fascinated with the sky. Early religions viewed the natural elements as manifestations of their gods; some cults even developed a surprising degree of sophistication in the science of astronomy. Stonehenge, the inexplicable monuments on the lonely Salisbury plains of England, is now thought to be a celestial observatory of incredible genius.

The *moon,* pale, aloof, and inconstant, reigns as queen of the celestial objects. The *moon in plenitude,* or *in her complement,* is a full moon depicted with a human face (Fig. 232). Partial moons, as shown in Figures 233, 240, and 241, are blazoned the moon in her *crescent, increscent,* and *decrescent* respectively. Stars, the night sky's mysterious companions, are blazoned as *estoiles* and, as shown in Figure 235, have six wavy rays. A star with straight lines (Fig. 237) is termed a *mullet* or *molet,* after the French "mollette" for a spur's rowel. The five-pointed star, used in our flag, has become virtually a national emblem, and is, therefore, a frequently used graphic element.

240   241

Among heavenly motifs, the most often used charge was the *sun*, symbol of life, light, and heat. The latter properties are indicated by eight straight rays for light, and eight wavy ones for heat. The sun with a human face (Fig. 243) is called *sun in his glory* (or *splendor*). However, when another charge replaces the human face, that charge is blazoned as *en soleil*. Figure 236 shows a white rose *en soleil*, the badge of the House of York. Sometimes the sun is shown emerging from behind clouds, with only its rays showing, as in Figure 234. Then it is called a *sunburst*. Among others, the sunburst was a badge of Richard II.

Figure 242 is the dreaded thunderbolt, depicted by a twisted column of flame between *cojoined* wings. This charge, with its jagged shafts of lightning, is marvelously contemporary in its symbolism. Electricity, for instance, is often depicted by lightning. As a design element, the thunderbolt charge conveys an image of immense power, literally one of dynamism.

Coming down to earth again, the oldest of the flora charges in heraldry is the *planta genista*, a broom plant. From this humble little plant (Fig. 238) stems one of history's famous names: it was because Geoffrey, Count of Anjou, wore a sprig of the broom plant in his cap that he was given the surname Plantagenet.

Heraldic plants are rarely shown in their entirety. Figure 244 is an exception: it is a tree *eradicated*, i.e., torn up from its roots, and *fructed*, i.e., bearing fruit. Figure 239 is a fructed dogwood. This charge is also *slipped* — an odd term meaning that the stem as well as the bloom is visible, while most heraldic plants are seen from above, showing only the bloom.

242

243

244

The *octofoil* (Fig. 245) was a popular flower charge probably derived from the shape of a strawberry flower. As the name indicates, it is shown with eight petals, but it can also be shown with four, five, or six, appropriately named *quatrefoil*, *cinquefoil*, and *sixfoil*.

The popular three-leaf clover (Fig. 246), called a *trefoil*, is the badge of Erin, emblem of St. Patrick and sign of luck. Because of its strong imagery, it has many applications.

Visually, the *oakleaf* (Fig. 247) is not as easily identifiable as is the trefoil. The *acorns*, however, make recognition easier and the association with the oak tree stronger. The sturdy oak was used as a charge because it has always symbolized strength and durability.

Some objects evoke an image that bears little resemblance to their actual character. For instance, the *thistle* (Fig. 248), identified with the charm of Scotland, where it is the national badge and an honorary order, is actually an obnoxious, prickly weed.

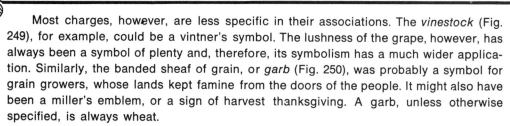

Most charges, however, are less specific in their associations. The *vinestock* (Fig. 249), for example, could be a vintner's symbol. The lushness of the grape, however, has always been a symbol of plenty and, therefore, its symbolism has a much wider application. Similarly, the banded sheaf of grain, or *garb* (Fig. 250), was probably a symbol for grain growers, whose lands kept famine from the doors of the people. It might also have been a miller's emblem, or a sign of harvest thanksgiving. A garb, unless otherwise specified, is always wheat.

Surrounding the garb is the *garland*, a romantic name for an entwined wreath of leaves or flowers. This versatile design element can be used to decorate almost any charge. A poignant version of a garland is the *Crown of Thorns*, symbol of the crucifixion (Fig. 251).

Of all the flower charges, the rose has been a perennial favorite, both for its romantic associations and for its enduring beauty. There are several different heraldic roses, some of which are shown above. Usually the rose has five petals, an inner rose (identical, but slightly turned), *barbs*, and a *seed pot*. When there is no inner rose, it is blazoned *plain*. The *slipped* and *leaved* rose is the plant badge of England. It is a combination of the Tudor rose of Henry VIII, who emerged from the ashes of the War of Roses, and the white and red roses of the ill-fated Yorks and Lancasters.

The *fleur-de-lis* has alway had strong associations with things French and, in fact, is the badge of France. It has been ever since the fifth century, when the first Clovis (an early form of Louis) claimed it was given to him by an angel at his baptism to Christianity. From this comes the interpretation "flower of Louis," though literally the name is translated "flower of the lily." The fleur-de-lis is a marvelous design element and probably the best known and most widely used floral symbol, both as a main charge and a decorative supplement to other charges. Page 68 shows only two of its many variations.

253

254

255

256

257

258

259

260

Man-Made Objects

Turning to the man-made world, heraldic designers found virtually an endless assortment of inanimate objects to adopt as charges. Such charges no doubt originated as pictorial representations, but many of them are no longer meaningful or even recognizable to us. Yet all of them offer interesting graphic forms that can well be used as design elements. For instance, the familiar bell: its origin as an heraldic charge is obscure, and it is simply termed either a *church bell* or a *war bell* (Fig. 254). This is not as incongruous as it seems, since the old church bells were used to rally the villagers to prepare for battle. Be that as it may, for modern designers the bell remains a decorative form of many meanings.

Easier identifications can be made with other objects, such as the *anchor* (Fig. 255). Its strong imagery makes the anchor easy to work with, but its overuse has made it a rather banal symbol unless the designer can breathe some style into it. The anchor shown is *cabled*, i.e., with a rope twisted around it.

In some cases, neither specific nor generalized associations are apparent. Figure 256 is an example. This charge is a *hawk's bell*, but unless it were so labeled, it would appear to most of us only as an attractive design form. In this manner, many everyday objects were developed by heraldic artists into wonderfully simple and decorative forms.

The *bridge* (Fig. 257) was not an uncommon charge. Like castles and cathedrals, bridges and towers were medieval landmarks and, in times of strife, strategic links to be taken or defended. Though their historical significance as charges has long since diminished, old bridges still carry with them a kind of nostalgic charm nurtured in us by romanticized legends. The *galley* (Fig. 258), sometimes referred to as a *lymphad* (the Gaelic word for longboat), is another charge that could very well feed on the romance in our imaginations. It fairly sings of adventure — of "the days when men were men" — a design concept that merchandisers of products for men have employed for years.

Often, several symbols are used in combination in order to tell a more precise story. Figure 259 shows three objects as charges: a quill, a book, and three crowns. The book, alone, could convey a number of thoughts — perhaps the bearer is a scholar, a librarian, or a bibliophile. But with the addition of a quill, the deduction that the bearer is an author of books is strongly suggested. Had the quill been used alone, it might have suggested writing — but not necessarily the writing of books. The crown could indicate a myriad of things — the writer may be a king; write about kings; write for a king; be named King or Crown, to mention a few. The variety of valid interpretations of a single symbol provides the designer with an enormous versatility in interpretation. Like semantic chameleons, countless symbols can assume different meanings with only the power of suggestion.

For example, *a wheel* as an heraldic charge is usually depicted as a wagon wheel, often with the kind of decorative spokes shown (Fig. 260). Yet suppose the wavy bar in the shield's base were said to represent the sea; could this change the wagon wheel into a ship's wheel? The designer has only to explore the potential of context to take full advantage of such forms.

Not all objects used as charges are lost in antiquity. Some objects are still very much in use today, for instance, the buckle (Fig. 261), called a *fermail* in the fifteenth century. Figure 262 resembles another familiar object, a glockenspiel. More accurately, it is a *Schellenbaum* — a tree of little bells that was mounted on the harness of sled horses. It is still often seen in marching bands and, even now, adorned with horsetails.

264

265

Of all the heraldic emblems that have come down through the ages, the *castle* is probably one of the most well known and often used charges of man-made objects. There is hardly a designer, heraldic or otherwise, who has not used, or considered using, a castle as a pictorial symbol. Figure 263 is a typical heraldic castle, depicted simply with two flat-topped towers connected by a high embattled wall with an arched gateway. Many variations of this charge are possible, for a castle remains a castle so long as it looks like one.

The door, or port, to the castle was protected by a *portcullis* (Fig. 264), which eventually became a separate charge in itself. A portcullis was a grid made of metal bars or heavy timbers bolted together. The bottom edge was armed with pointed spikes to discourage those attackers who attempted a last minute dash into the castle before the falling portcullis secured the gateway. The heavy rings and chains used to raise the device are usually included in this charge. The portcullis symbol, said to have originally been a sign of gratitude to a host for providing refuge for a king, was worn as an additional element on the bearer's shield. Eventually, it became a reward for any faithful deed. (This and other *augmentations* are shown in Appendix F).

272   273   274

275   276   277

Keys were also used as additional elements on shields. Keys *in saltire*, i.e., crossed (Fig. 265), are important in ecclesiastical heraldry; Saint Peter used keys as his emblem. Graphically, the key, with its varied connotations and strong visual identity, has good design potential today, since technology of all sorts is "unlocking" the secrets of man and nature.

Weapons of war have always held a prominent place in heraldry. From the time of the Crusades, weapons have been shown in various ways as distinguishing badges, emblems, or symbols — the forerunners of modern military insignia. A surprising number of classical military heraldic charges is still used today. Actually, many of the medieval weapons are also found as symbols in other applications, without military connotations, and far removed from their original purpose. For instance, the *halberd* (Fig. 266), used by foot soldiers to unseat mounted warriors, was a vicious weapon that combined a spearlike pike with a battle-ax. But for all its ferocity, it has exceptional graphic possibilities, especially when stylized and made highly ornamental. Thus, halberds, reminiscent of pomp, pageantry, and battle, are natural design symbols for things masculine.

Arrows (Fig. 267) were universal weapons of war. Heraldic designers used parts or all of the arrow, in various combinations. Though the arrow was primarily an instrument of death, the pure line of its shaft, coupled with the angularity of its head and its feathered tail, has always made it a design favorite. Also, time has added associations like "true," "Cupid," and "straight" to the arrow's real identity, thereby neutralizing its original meaning. A similar observation can be made about the *sword*, shown with a crown in Figure 268. This combination suggests strength, or regal power, rather than a weapon of war. The *crossbow* (Fig. 269), more a weapon of yeomen than of knights, was an exceedingly dangerous device. Its outlines are so graphically powerful that many interesting patterns can be developed. Also interesting as a design form is the *caltrap* (Fig. 270), an ancient weapon that is little known today. This nasty contraption, an iron ball with three metal spikes, was thrown on the battlefield before the battle started in order to incapacitate a horse so that it threw its knight. Caltraps were often used as charges, probably because the knight was victorious through the use of this ancient "land mine" or was particularly adept at avoiding them.

Chess, the ancient game of war, was also represented in charges. The *chess knight* (Fig. 271), developed as a piece in the fifteenth century, is shown adorned with a fetterlock (a shackle and padlock), which often appeared alone as a charge.

Figures 272, 273, and 274 are a few different examples of the *clarion* — a very old musical wind instrument used by shepherds and by the mythical Pan. In all its variations, the clarion is a beautiful form. Similarly, Figures 275, 276, and 277 are three of the many *millrind* variations. A millrind was an iron clamp used to hold two millstones in place; it was fashioned in countless striking forms by the medieval blacksmiths who forged them. Many landowners adopted these forms as badges and used them on their liveries, sacks, and wagons, much as we use trademarks today.

The *carbuncle* (Fig. 278) was originally a reinforcement for the center of a shield. Consisting of eight decorated metal bands hubbed with a boss, carbuncles were painted in different colors and were the predecessors of the ordinaries and charges. It, too, takes on many forms, as did the *water bouget* (Fig. 279), which was made of two leather bags or pig bladders mounted on a wooden crosspiece and used to transport water or wine.

And, finally, there were the many forms of the *manche* (Fig. 280), a strange charge indeed. This Gothic sleeve with a hanging lappet supposedly belonged to one's admired damsel, and was carried as a sign of love and devotion. (It was a very romantic and sentimental age.)

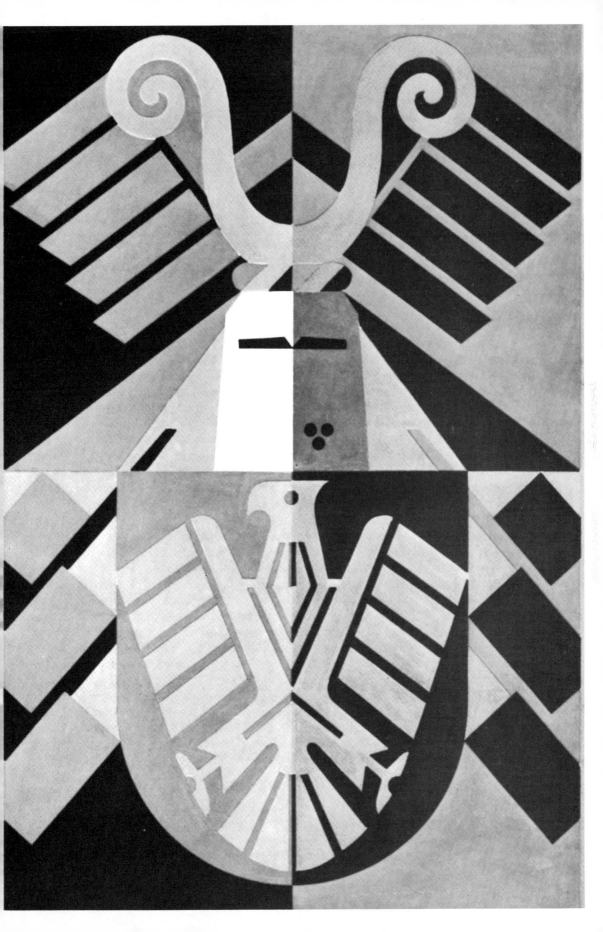

Changing STYLES

Like all artistic creations, coats of arms have been closely tied to the style of their times. By the middle of the thirteenth century, the development of heraldic concepts had stabilized, but, stylistically, the renditions remained charmingly primitive. It was not until the early Gothic style came of age that heraldry evolved into a captivating art form. From then on, changing heraldic styles parallel the great periods of art and, graphically, tell some interesting stories.

The arms opposite tell one such story, which begins about 1300. The helmet is a primitive form of pothelm without a coat. The shield, shaped like an inverted pointed gothic arch, shows eagles in an angry fighting mood. Let us say the arms belonged to a powerful knight, represented by the main eagle. Unfortunately, his two quarreling sons did not see eye to eye, though they are shown that way on the shield.

By 1350 the knight had died, and his realm was divided, reflected in the new arms by a bend-sinster. Blue was introduced as a compromise to a strong second son, who was forced to relinquish the larger share because of the rights, primogeniture, of his older brother. In style, little has changed, but a mantle was added.

Some hundred years later, the descendants of the older son took over completely, and through intermarriages, like the modern mergers, five estates were brought into the family. The late Gothic rendition shows the first major change both in style and content. Symbols of the merged houses appear in the crest. For the first time a torse appears, securing a comparatively elaborate mantle. The helmet is more realistic, the shield rounded. The lone eagle is shown with an inescutcheon adorned by a heart — the symbol of the wife's family, which also appears in the crest.

By 1500 the blue Lion's family has made substantial inroads into the main family, and this progress is duly noted by the demi-lion in base under the chevron and, more significantly, by half the mantle being made blue. Early Renaissance enrichment of the arms is seen in the mantle's flowing styling. The great tilting helm, with its polished curves and heavy chest fastenings, is introduced; and the shield, no longer tilted, is notched to suggest provisions for a lance. Most characteristic of the period are the wings as the crest.

A century and a half later, the blue Lion's family was rewarded for its perseverance by marrying into the main red Eagle family. The two most important families now shared the shield by impalement. The hearts remained as a badge between the crest of wings. The style, late Renaissance, is the most elaborate in the entire development of classical arms. The mantle is decoratively massive. The helm, the most ornate so far, is crowned by a crest of wings about to take flight.

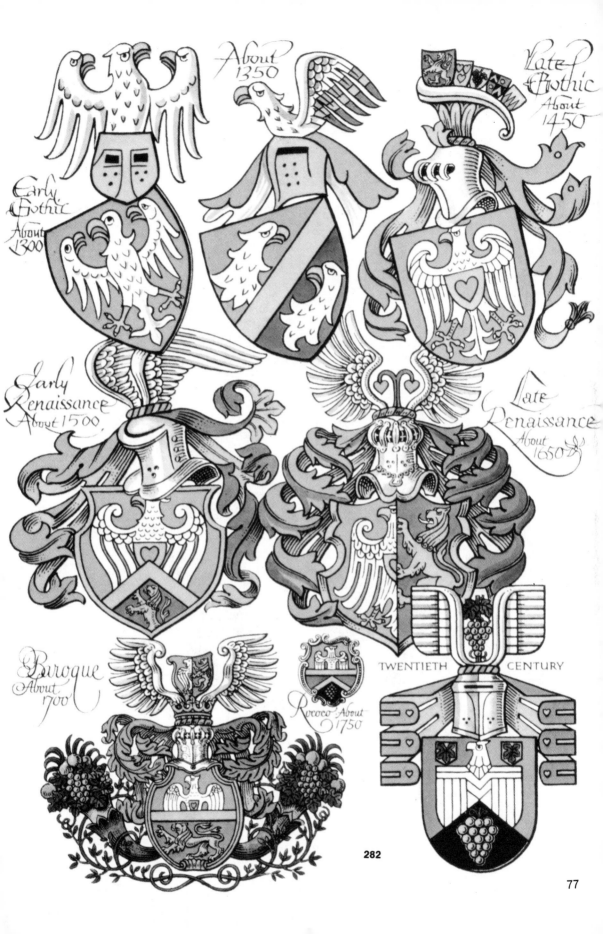

About 1350

Late Gothic
About 1450

Early Gothic
About 1300

Early Renaissance
About 1500

Late Renaissance
About 1650

Baroque
About 1700

Rococo About 1750

TWENTIETH CENTURY

282

77

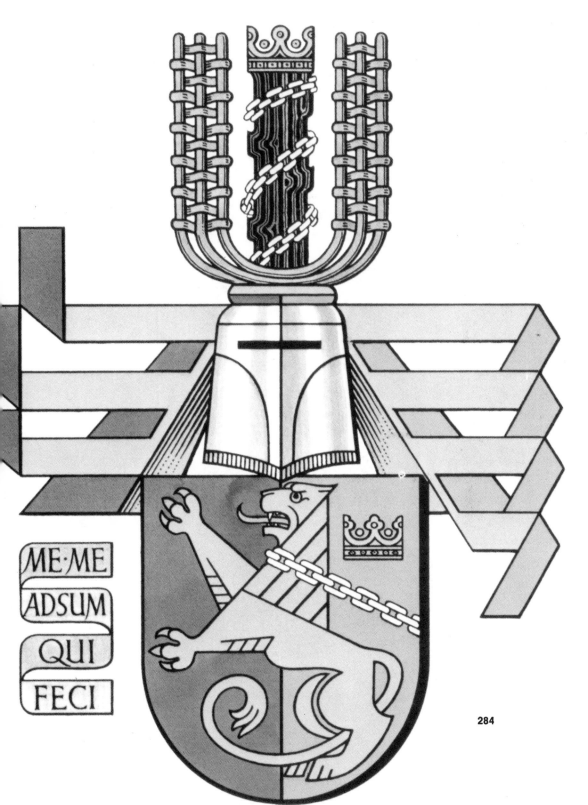

ME·ME
ADSUM
QUI
FECI

284

285

Only two generations later, the arms were changed, not so much in content, but extravagantly in form. The baroque, with all its grandiose ornamentation, took hold. The concept of the coat of arms declined, the design becoming overloaded with adornments that negate heraldry's classic purpose by smothering the contents of the shield. The badge of hearts is gone, replaced with the impaled arms. The helmet has lost none of its gaudiness, and is graced with a crown of some pretension. An oval shield is introduced, and on it the lion appears suspiciously tamed. And, for the first time, the grape family appears, shown in the cornucopias.

The rococo period, though also marked by a florid style of ornamentation, cleared away much of the too playful baroque. The Grape family has increased in prominence, supplanting the Lion, from which only the blue survived.

Some three hundred years later, as our story comes to a close, the Grape family remains, sharing the shield with the Eagle of the original main family, and dominating the crest. Two grape leaves adorn the impaled shield, partially blue in remembrance of times passed. The symbol of the heart is also retained and now embellishes the mantle. Stylistically, the design of the arms has reverted to the clear and powerful expression of the early Gothic simplicity, and the coat of arms has closed the circle of changing styles.

In retrospect, however, a commentary on the hiatus that lasted over a century after the exuberant style changes of the eighteenth century is necessary. Long before this time, the Galileos and Newtons had been steadily contributing to a considerable reservoir of scientific knowledge, although little practical use had been made of it. Soon, however, the gnawing restlessness of industrialization threw open the sluices; knowledge was harnessed to application, and the scientific era gained its momentum. The force of this flood pushed art from the forefront of men's minds; and so began a standstill — even a depressing decline — in the fields of style and design.

Not until the end of the nineteenth century did a new awakening occur. Men began seeking new kinds of expression in architecture, painting, and industrial design. French painters and English, Austrian, and German designers, clearing away the cobwebs of redundancy and the deadwood of outmoded tradition, started to make a new beginning. In the wake of this countersurge, the twentieth century rejuvenated heraldry as an art. Perhaps most characterized by its simplicity of form, modern heraldry has rigorously pruned the three-dimensional pictorialization of the Renaissance and baroque periods and has returned to the two-dimensional expression so typical of the Gothic style. Three examples of such contemporary treatments follow.

On page 78 is an unusual form of a coat of arms called a *tent.* It has no helmet, and uses a coat, or mantle, as a carrier of the shield, crown, and sword. It is a royal bearing that signifies the feudal combination of church and state. Modernization is accomplished mainly by the simplification of the mantle.

Page 79 shows a contemporary rendition of conventional arms of an imaginary individual instrumental in divesting his country of a mighty alien power, symbolized by the lion. *Chained* and *cowed* (i.e., its tail between its legs), the lion is now the main charge of the victor. The crest is fashioned of the device used to hold back the earth of battle trenches, and the *raguly* tree, crowned, signifies the withered might of the former oppressor.

And finally, opposite, is a garter decorated with fleur-de-lis and surrounding the legendary phoenix rising from the ashes. This rendition is a modern adaptation of the Order of the Garter and could well serve as a colorful hanging or a tablecloth of state.

MEA PARVITAS

Personal Arms

Heraldry, born in the Middle Ages and flowering during the Renaissance, is generally considered an art of the past. Invariably, heraldic terms like mantle, shield, and helmet bring to mind charging knights on a field of battle. Improbable creatures like dragons, rampant lions, and two-headed eagles can only have belonged to the credulous age of chivalry. And psychologically, the coat of arms, long considered the hallmark of aristocracy, is an anomaly in a democracy.

For such reasons there exists a popular conception that heraldry is a dead art. But it is an erroneous one, for the art of heraldry is alive and well, and living here in America.

By and large, new and old heraldic devices are found in numerous commercial applications, such as corporate and brand identities. But there is also an ever-growing field of modern heraldry used for heraldic purposes, and the creative coin gained from working with "living" coats of arms can present an exciting venture for any designer.

Essentially, there are two routes by which a designer can become involved in this field of heraldry. The first is working with an ancestral coat of arms handed down to a descendant, from which one or a combination of assignments can result. In some cases the client may merely wish to have the arms reproduced from a static medium (e.g., a tapestry, or perhaps a woodcut, like the one shown at left) so that it can be used in various other applications. Often, he may take the liberty of personalizing the arms by adding or subtracting elements to reflect his generation rather than those of the past. And in some cases he may wish to change the heirloom's existing style to one more correct or contemporary in its graphic treatment.

The second route, that of designing an original insignia, using bona fide heraldic methodology, is indeed a challenge. A modern coat of arms, like its predecessors, is conceived as a visual communication depicting one or more ideas. The arms could be a pictorial representation or a rebus of the client's name, or portray some signal accomplishment. His vocation and/or avocation is often used as the primary or secondary theme. And sometimes a notable event or personage in his heritage, or even from the lineage of his spouse, is included in the design of his coat of arms.

On the pages that follow I have shown some of the personal coats of arms I have designed that serve to illustrate the designer's role in modern heraldry.

The coat of arms above was designed for Dr. Clarence Bartlett. The name Bartlett appeared to be a diminutive of "bart" — for which I could find no meaning. Using another approach, I found that the name identifies a variety of pear, introduced into this country long ago by one Enoch Bartlett. Although our Bartlett was not related, I nevertheless felt that the association of the Bartlett name with the pear was semantically strong enough to use a pear tree as the main charge. Although no link to Enoch was known, our Bartlett does believe he is somehow connected to one Josiah Bartlett who was, coincidentally, a noted physician, and a prominent New England patriot in the Revolutionary War. Since the precise connection to Josiah was somewhat tenuous, I was reluctant to incorporate his arms; circumstantially, however, there was reason enough to include an inescutcheon symbolizing early Americana.

Dr. Bartlett's profession was easily handled by using a caduceus as the base of the crest. Stylistically, the graphic treatment of the tree, its oversized leaves and pears, and the handling of the grass in the base are typical of modern heraldry.

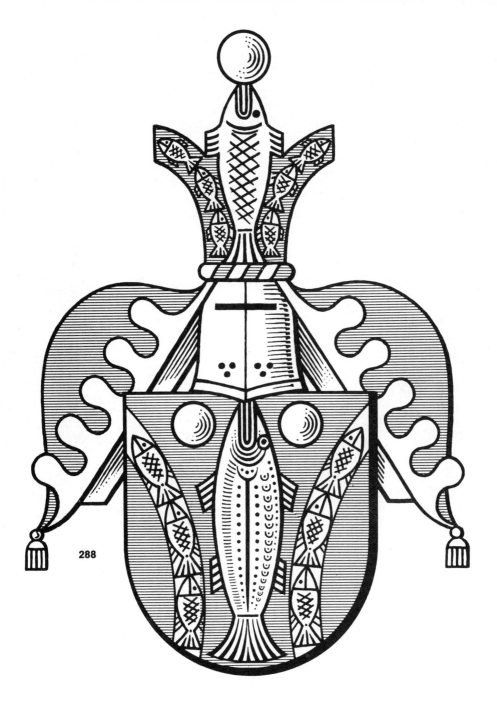

288

Pictorially, depicting the name Fischel was much more direct; Fischel means "little fish," and so it was immediately apparent that a fish would become the main charge. With equal immediateness two problems came into focus. The first was that "little" is a comparative term; the second was that some implications of "a little fish" were derogatory, and therefore "fish" must be construed in the plural.

The solution, as shown in the coat of arms above, was to use a larger fish as a frame of reference in depicting a school of "little fish." The crest repeats the idea. As an added measure, an abstract fishnet was styled as a mantle.

The two roundels in chief and the one capping the crest are very subtle embellishments. They are meant to represent tennis balls, for Mr. Fischel is a passionate devotee of the game; in his sixties, he continues to play regularly.

289

The name Swanson provided a number of approaches to designing a coat of arms. The rendition shown above is one of the variations I submitted to my client. I have included it to demonstrate the sometimes convoluted rationales used in formulating a design.

Firstly, the thought of devising a rebus by using the sun in place of "son" together with a swan was instantly rejected as banal. The swan alone could pictorially depict Swanson — a solution quite adequate, but not literally accurate. Literally, the "son of Swan" needed a parent of whom it was a son. Thus the design had to incorporate a big swan and a little swan. But how? Certainly if "*son* of swan," and not "*little* swan," was to be the theme, some sort of parent-child relationship should come through.

My solution was to place the little swan piggyback on the big swan, thereby pictorially implying the kind of belonging, or dependence, that relate child and parent. And so quite satisfied, I arrived at Swanson. Yet inevitably, I was later asked whether the roundel in sinister chief was just a design, or was it supposed to be the sun, "like in Swan-sun."

The highly stylized rooster in the modern coat of arms shown at right could very well be the symbol for a family named Hahn. In German, Hahn means "rooster," and I know a Hahn family, but this was not done for them. Nor was it done for a poultry raiser, or alarm-clock-maker, or even a lothario. It is a liquor label; in fact, a play on words, for the cock looking at his tail is meant to say *cocktail*. It is one of several designs of a label symbol for Heublein Club Cocktails which I did several years ago. I have included it here as additional evidence of the marvelous range of applicability of heraldic arms.

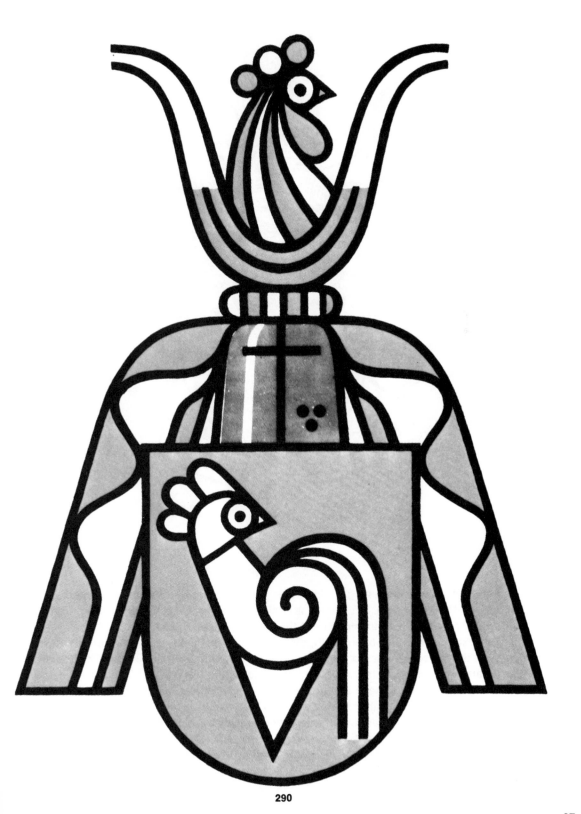

290

Nec Gladio — Nec Arco

One of my most interesting assignments was restoring and refurbishing the ancestral arms of Harold Dudley. Mr. Dudley is a direct descendant of Robert Dudley, Earl of Leicester, who was a famous member of the court of Queen Elizabeth I.

The extant arms had been badly distorted and artistically spoiled during the last century, but with some research we were fortunate enough to find the original Leicester coat of arms tucked away in the upper left corner of one of the Earl's portraits. Using that as a guide, I tried to save as much of the original form as possible.

The major problem with the existing arms was that it lacked authenticity, and this points up the gross disadvantage of attempting to design a coat of arms without a working knowledge of the rudiments of heraldry. In this particular case the relative proportions between crest and shield were wrong, and the formulation of the mantle was totally misunderstood.

Fortunately, however, finding the original coat of arms provided the necessary background from which the armorial bearings of this particular branch of the Dudley family could be reconstructed.

292

The reconstruction of some old heirlooms can really be fascinating, as illustrated by the redesign of the ancestral arms of Dr. Otto Schwarz. All that remained to show his family coat of arms was a signet ring handed down through the generations. The face of the ring was worn and difficult to see, even under a microscope. Patiently I pieced the elements together, identifying all but the crest with reasonable certainty. The crest was almost entirely obliterated, but enough remained to conclude that it had once been an animal — perhaps either a lion or an enfield.

Despite this uncertainty, I proceeded with the redesign, deciding to retain the Renaissance helm and mantle and clean up the shield. The crest remained a puzzle until an important clue was uncovered. As it turned out, Dr. Schwarz had in his possession an etching of the old family home in Alsace; above its door was a lion. That clinched it; I made the crest a lion.

293

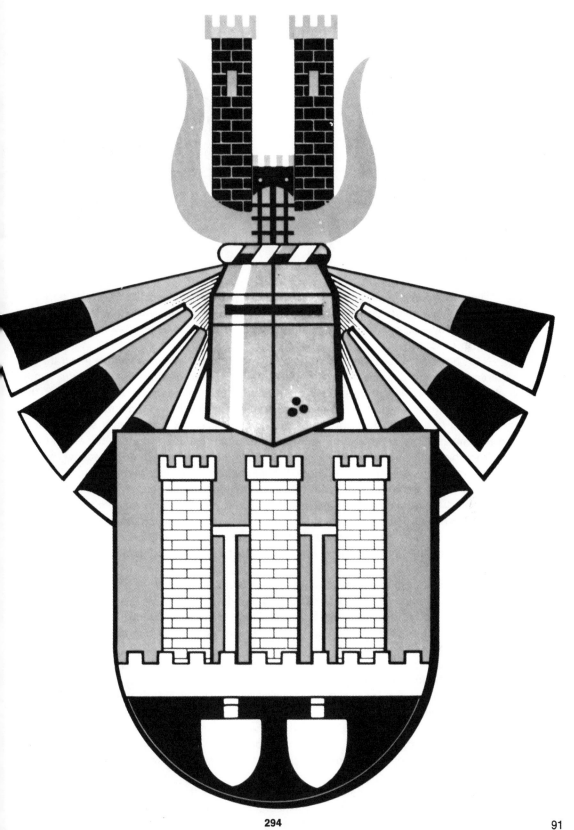

294

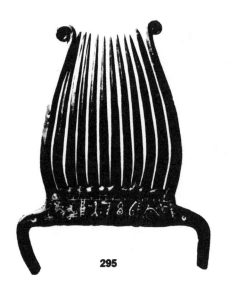

295

296

There is a very good and admired friend of mine, Professor Dr. H. G. Hillebrecht, for whom I have designed not one, but two coats of arms. Unfortunately, the good professor has never asked for either one, and I could never tell him they lay in a drawer waiting to be born.

Now, however, I have decided to use them because they serve well to illustrate the difference in doing a family arms and a very personal coat of arms. Let's take the family first. With some investigation I found the name Hillebrecht reaches as far back as the late Middle Ages; it was coined in a small village in northern Germany as a mark of special skill in combing flax efficiently and quickly. The flax plants were slammed into the fine mesh of the comb's teeth and pulled through fast and forcefully to separate the flax from the chaff and strip off the seed. Since "hille" means fast, and "brecht," breaking, the name was created to describe "the man who breaks flax fast and efficiently."

A bit more research in a local museum provided some pictures of really beautiful combs used for breaking flax. One, a wrought-iron piece of arm mounted on a heavy wooden base (Fig. 298), was very decorative but looked too much like a lyre. A simpler comb (Fig. 296) was better suited. Thus, I put flax plants behind the comb indicating what was "brecht," and a bird on wing as a crest so as to emphasize the swiftness in "hille."

The second, personal coat of arms for my friend denotes a signal achievement of his, for which he has received international attention and acclaim. Professor Hillebrecht was the architect solely responsible for rebuilding the city of Hannover from the vast mountain of rubble it was at the end of the war. His work made him famous, and it was this achievement that I chose for his personal arms.

The design approach I took was a bit different. Whereas the crest's charge usually repeats the shield's charge, or sometimes amplifies the main charge — as, for example, where the bird is used for the "hille" symbolism — the charge on this crest serves as "before," as compared to the shield's charge which serves as "after." The before-charge of the crest is an adaptation of Hannover's arms (page 100). Only the castle is used, its two towers blackened and charred, its portcullis closed. The horns are replaced by flames. The after-charge of the shield shows new towers: three this time, to indicate architectural progress, and embattled to indicate the preservation of the city's old style and charm. The spades, of course, symbolize the herculean task of clearing away the rubble. This coat of arms had special significance for me: not only is the good professor my dear friend, but Hannover is my home town.

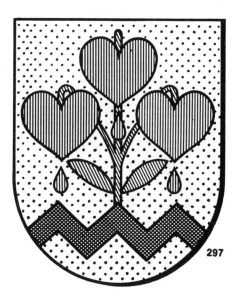

297

Many years ago I decided that my family would not be like that of the shoemaker: we would have a coat of arms. I considered a number of approaches. My father's ancestors were artisans of one type or another, and that offered a number of possibilities. Also, I considered my mother's family, which was steeped in tradition dating back to before Napoleon's time, when a father of a father of a father in my mother's clan was Master of the Horses for no less a personage than a king. This tradition, I felt, should prevail. Her family name was the Flemish "Ryssel," which is some sort of tree sprout — a kind of little leaf coming out of a branch. Determining what kind of sprout I should use was comparatively easy, because a favorite family plant was the tiny blossom of a small shrub called the "bleeding heart." So this became the main badge of the family arms. The three hearts in the arms above represented my sister, my brother, and myself. To represent my father I chose another symbol, the dancetty line at the base of the shield. I chose it because it best depicted the charmer my father was; truly a *bon vivant*, he was an endless fountain of cheer and gaity.

But now all that has passed, and I have recently changed our family arms. I am the last of the Metzig line, and on the next page I have tried to depict this by showing the tree as withered. The two new hearts are my grandchildren through my daughter who married a Burg. The hearts are therefore charged with castles, for that is the meaning of their name.

The symbolism incorporated into a coat of arms should never remain static, but continually change, to tell the story as it it is today.

Probably the oddest personal arms I ever designed belongs to a remarkable young man who, as far as I know, has never displayed it, yet has kindly allowed me to use it here, on page 95. This coat of arms is not based on a pictorial representation of his name. Nor has it anything to do with his vocation or avocation. And there is nothing ancestral about the use of a wyvern as his symbol.

The wyvern represents what was once this man's "personal dragon" — something against which he had waged an agonizing battle most of his adult life. Fortunately he won the battle; he slew his dragon. And this feat is what the arms commemorates. The crest victoriously shows the decapitated monster, as ugly in death as it must have been in life. The tilted shield, still caught in the frenzy of motion, shows the once insatiable demon cut to pieces from a fury only vengeance can know. Finally, the mantle, draped darkly over the elongated helm like a pall anchored by its gloomy tassels, is to him symbolic of the melancholy he once endured — a grim reminder of his past life. Indeed, heraldic arms can sometimes fill some strange roles.

299

EX LIBRIS

EXITUS ACTA PROBAT

300

A growing application of personal heraldic arms is in *ex libris.* Quantitatively, American reading is greater than that of any other nation. If John Doe is not a book reader, chances are he may still be a book owner, for through the irresistible institution of book clubs, millions of homes now have a "library" — some of them of considerable dimension.

Many generations ago, when books were few, and their possession rare, each volume was dearly prized by its owner. To be allowed to borrow a book was a privilege with which few were honored. As a sign of pride and, discreetly, of ownership, bookplates were used. These were labels bearing the owner's name and pasted on the book's front endpaper. Normally, bookplates were decorative; very often they were adaptations of family coats of arms, such as the one above belonging to George Washington.

As the number of personal libraries grew, and the practice of borrowing likewise increased, the phrase "ex libris" before the owner's name began appearing on bookplates. Taken from the Latin, and literally meaning "from the library of," the term has gradually replaced "bookplate," and today is used in lieu of it.

The elk antler, shown as the main charge of an ex libris done for Dora Deves, has actually been the family badge for centuries. The origin of the badge is unknown, but I speculated that her ancestors were once huntsmen, and so I added a crest of trees to represent a forest. My speculation is somewhat supported by the military tradition in her family, which is indicated by a sword.

The ex libris with a rooster is not a liquor label — it is for the Hahn family.

Robert Maller is a banker whose green thumb is at home both counting the till and tilling the soil. The roundels are ancient symbols for money, the plants stand for gardening, and his two children are represented by the split tree.

The family name of Matthew Murgio, unlike many Sicilian names, has no known meaning, nor is it associated with any locale. The castles in the shield represent "Costello," his mother's name. The small weights in the base are a pictorial translation of "routala" (weight) — an ancient appellation given his father's family in its native town. The ex libris is personalized by the addition of a lyre and quill to represent his long standing interest in composing music.

Ex Libris

301

Dora Deves

303

EX LIBRIS

KARIN HAHN

302

EX LIB

ROBERT MALLER

304

EX LIB

MURGIO

305

306

OFFICIAL INSIGNIA

The use of armorial bearings by institutions exercising authority is probably the principal field in which traditional heraldic design remains almost unaltered. The stature and dignity vested in these heraldic arms has come down to us from the times of kings, and represents the essence of officialdom. By and large, however, these arms, seals, and badges are in desperate need of modernization to clear away the clutter imposed by eighteenth and nineteenth century designers. As such, the opportunity for redesign is immense.

For instance, at left is a modernization in line form of the American seal. Above is still a further abstraction in a massive treatment. In both cases I have tried not to violate the essence of the original concept in my redesign.

On the following page is the coat of arms of the city of Hannover. In 1930 I did this redesign by clearing away the old, somewhat cluttered original that had no particular style. I developed a new line of "main," "medium," and "small" emblems, modernized the seals, and designed the official stationery. A main coat of arms is always shown with supporters; it is sometimes called the "great" arms — it is the official one (Fig. 329). The medium arms has no supporters or ribbons, and the small one has only the shield without helm or crest.

Figure 308 could be the coat of arms of a small fishing village, perhaps on the Mediterranean. In this case the three fish refer to the great catch of fish — "one hundred and fifty-three" made by Saint Peter in the seas of Tiberia.

307

308

309

SEQUERE DEUM

310

SEQUERE DEUM

311

The ecclesiastical coat of arms, top left, belonged to the late Cardinal Spellman of New York. It contained many different forms of crosses, and a wide variety of other insignia, the most important being the patriarchial cross, top center; the pastoral staff, at sinister; and the mitre in dexter. As a cardinal, his arms had fifteen tassels on two cords coming out of a bishop's hat. All the elements were traditionally founded. Unfortunately, however, the overall design is very busy.

Below it is my redesign, in which I have tried to rearrange the elements to achieve a clearer and better appearance. I omitted the pastoral staff to give more prominence to the mitre — the symbol ensigned to all bishop's arms — and also to allow an orderly arrangement of the traditional hat and tassels. The patriarchial cross was moved onto the shield as the main charge. All other charges, except the maltese cross, remain, and, although repositioned, are heraldically sound.

Prior to heraldic arms, bishops' seals served as ecclesiastical insignia, and many have prevailed. The one above belongs to the Bishop of Louisiana; it is a particularly excellent one. The star and plough in chief symbolize his work in the fields of heaven. The pelican has a dual significance: it is Louisiana's state bird and, vulning itself, it is the symbol of the Eucharist in ecclesiastical heraldry. In this marvelous seal I only modified the border and indicated a red tincture in chief.

Historically, the first commercial applications of pictorial identification were the guild symbols of the Middle Ages. Although these "marks of trade" were instituted for a populace largely illiterate, their usefulness eventually became the basis from which the modern trademark was developed.

The guilds were powerful forces that managed, through their monopoly of commerce, virtually to dominate society and its governments for centuries. So great was their prestige that their signs were looked upon as official emblems.

Many of the guild symbols are still used. Below is an excellent old guild sign found on the front of Carpenter's Hall in Philadelphia.

The illustration at right makes use of the main tools of the printing trade, rollers and pads. It is part of the title page of a folder I designed for a 150-year-old printing plant. Since it was a promotion folder, I chose the style of the ancient guilds as the one most fitting to represent this old and well known establishment.

The coat of arms on page 106 was designed as the official insignia of the Kew Forest Art School. In it I have tried to capture both the essence of the school and a pictorial representation of its name. The highly stylized trees, of course, symbolize the forest, while the pencil in the crest and the paint brush in the shield suggest the art.

Insignias like this one differ from trademarks in that they represent entities dedicated to the public interest — no matter how small — rather than commercial enterprises producing only consumer products.

Many profit and nonprofit institutions, associations, and organizations fall into this category, and merit being treated as "official" bodies; all of them should have appropriate insignia to represent them.

312

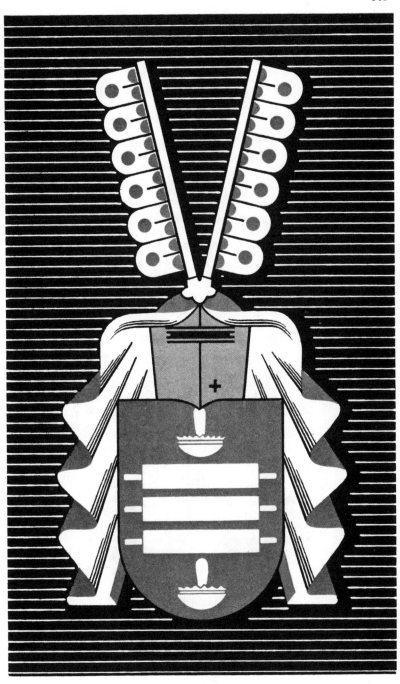

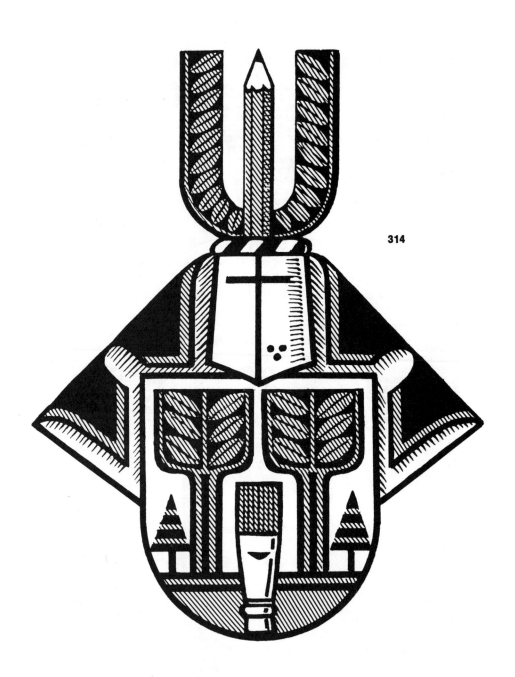

314

COMMERCIAL APPLICATIONS

The boom of new business entities over the last decade and the proliferation of multiple product lines in existing businesses have created a vast market for design services. The former are in need of distinctive identity symbols, and the latter of creative packaging design that will "sell" the consumer the product they contain. Heraldic design, effective for both purposes, offers the designer a virtually limitless source of ideas in meeting today's demand for his services.

In the illustrations that follow, I have tried to show some of the commercial applications I have drawn from heraldic design.

Below is a neck label for a new brand of Canadian whiskey. Richly embossed, it suggests a product "fit for a king." The Royal Arms of England are alluded to, but *never* copied exactly, since that is not permitted.

315

Following the same line of thought, a double eagle, the emblem of the Russian tsars, was used as the centerpiece of the above vodka label done for Heublein, Inc. In both cases I felt that the classic heraldic devices would serve the purpose of identification best.

At right is a trademark designed for a manufacturer of alligator and lizard handbags. Pertinent in concept and playful in execution, it is an easy symbol to remember — which is the first criterion for a trademark. The lizard is an old heraldic charge that has been denuded here of its customary gruesomeness.

DEITSCH

318

319

Figure 318 was done for a brewery. It is a sun with a crown fashioned from three cones of hops around an ear of malt. While beer is not considered a particularly royal brew, there has always been a rivalry among brewers to produce the "king of beers" — hence the crown.

The colophon shown in Figure 319 is a phoenix "growing out of" the letter *W*. It was part of a study for John Wiley & Sons, publishers of technical books. I chose the phoenix, symbol of eternal rejuvenation, as a most appropriate symbol for science.

The griffin-like creature (Fig. 320) was designed as a trademark for Koudelka Photomounts. The griffin, as you know, is part eagle and part lion; here I shaped the wings to form a *K*.

The design in Figure 321 was prepared for an aircraft manufacturer, and demonstrates the possibility of "inventing" a new charge. Here the characteristics of an eagle are combined with those of a human figure to symbolize man's age-old dream to fly.

At right is a design for a promotional piece for Tietgen Research Associates, a marketing firm. The design was developed out of the wings and the arrow of the president's coat of arms, used here as a badge in both wings. The arrow feathered by wings presents a dynamic symbolism which characterizes the aspirations of the firm.

320

321

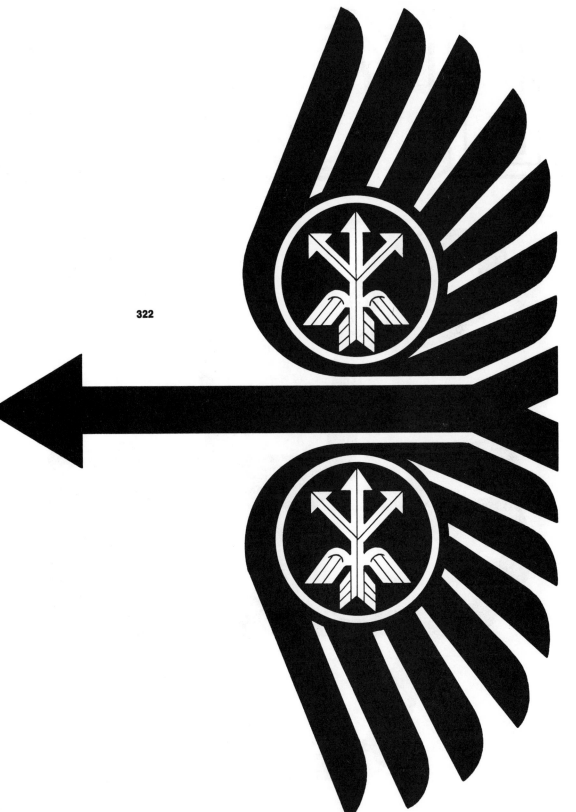

322

324

Above is that fellow Pan in full action (musically, that is). I did this rendition of an old heraldic symbol as part of a design study for NBC Radio years ago.

Left is an application of one of my favorite heraldic charges, the lion, for a book jacket.

IMPERATOR

326

327

On page 114 is a king of spades from a deck of playing cards I designed many years ago. It was a difficult, but rewarding, design assignment in which familiarity with heraldic elements was an invaluable aid — no designer should be without it in attempting such a task. Playing cards have been in use since the Middle Ages and have changed over the centuries according to prevailing styles. Almost always rich in ornamentation, they incorporated many well-known charges such as leaves, crowns, flowers, lines and ordinaries, trefoils, hearts, and representations of kings and queens.

Page 115 shows an emperor wearing his regalia in all its splendor. He is mounted on a horse with its *trappings*, a coat embroidered with royal badges or main charge, covering the whole horse. This piece was designed as a cover for a brand of printing inks called Imperator. The copious use of detail and extravagant use of color in the design provided an excellent showcase for the richness and variety of the company's inks.

Above, in black and white, is a stylized rendition of a soaring bird of paradise whose very colorful tail is fashioned into a button. It is a trademark for nothing less than a maker of very colorful buttons, and an apt illustration of the fact that a company's image today serves the same purpose as did the charges on the knight's shield of long ago: to identify him in the milieu of his time.

Thus, the purpose of identity remains, but so do the problems of communicating it. Those designers who turn to the old art of heraldry will be rewarded, for they will find it by no means out of fashion — the old *bougets* can well be filled with a new and sparkling wine.

328

Acknowledgments

A number of people helped launch this book, and it is with pleasure and gratitude that I acknowledge their contributions.

Klaus Burg deserves the credit for working out the concept of the book with me; his encouragement was most valuable.

Then, the tireless efforts of Matthew Murgio and my daughter Beatrice Burg are responsible for effectively organizing and editing my manuscript. They spent many hours in researching facts and fancies to support and augment the technical material I prepared.

Other contributors helped in various ways, and these acknowledgments would not be complete without giving thanks to Stanley Hauser, Dr. Robert Leslie, Ewald van Elken, and Chrissy Harris for access to their libraries.

Finally, my thanks go to my wife Erica, who shared with me the years of trials and tribulations while I designed this book.

THE ELEMENTS

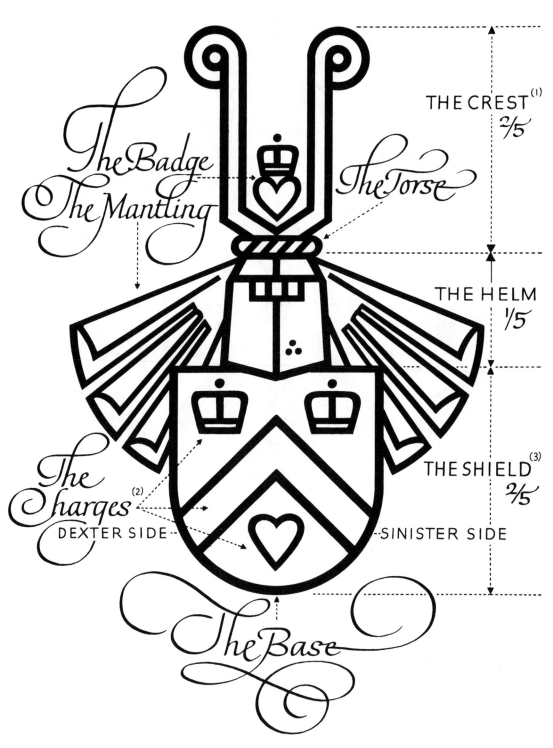

THE CREST [1]
2/5

The Badge
The Mantling

The Torse

THE HELM
1/5

THE SHIELD [3]
2/5

The Charges [2]

DEXTER SIDE

SINISTER SIDE

The Base

(1) When there is a lack of space to accommodate the crest's full proportion, it can be made smaller. (2) The area of any charge should fill its field as completely as possible. (3) An important general rule to follow is *no color on color* (e.g. red on green), and *no metal on metal* (i.e. gold on silver), whether in the shield or in the mantle.

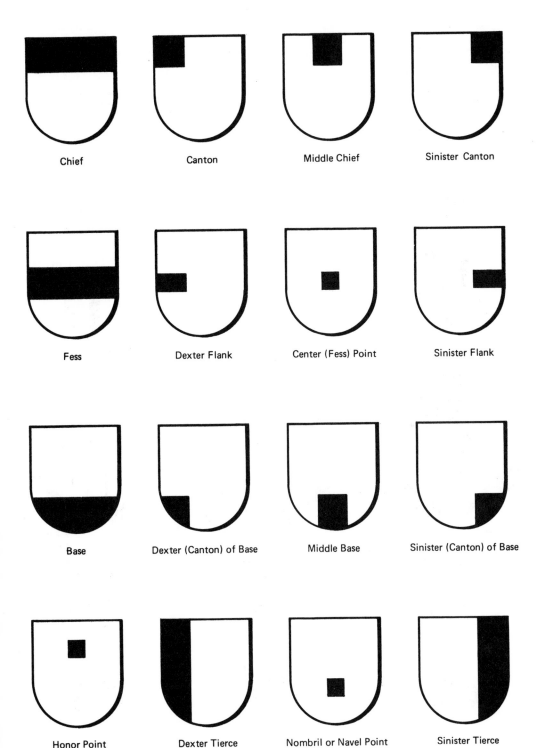

Chief · Canton · Middle Chief · Sinister Canton

Fess · Dexter Flank · Center (Fess) Point · Sinister Flank

Base · Dexter (Canton) of Base · Middle Base · Sinister (Canton) of Base

Honor Point · Dexter Tierce · Nombril or Navel Point · Sinister Tierce

Proportioning Guidelines of Ordinaries

Since the beginning of heraldry, the proportioning of ordinaries and their diminutives have been left to the discretion of the artist and thus, there exist no precise rules. Below, however, are those generally accepted guidelines most frequently used in heraldic design.

Primary ordinaries fill *not more* than 1/3 and *not less* than 1/5 the height or width of the shield.	First diminutives and some uncharged primary ordinaries fill *not more* than 1/5 and *not less* than 1/6 the height or width of the shield.	Second diminutives are 1/2 the width of their respective primary or first diminutive ordinary.

Chief

Fess

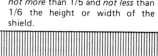

Bar

Closet

Pale

Pallet

Primaries, Charged

Primaries, Uncharged

Cross

Cross

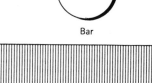

Bend　　　Bend Sinister

Bend　　　Bend Sinister

Bendlet, *charged*　　Scarp

Saltire

Saltire

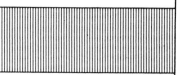

Salterol

Chevron

Chevron

Chevronnel, *charged*

The *cotise* (called an *endorse* when used with a pale) is a third diminutive that is 1/2 the width of its respective first or second diminutive.

Position Names for Lions and other animals	Attitude of body	Position of paws	Position of Head	Position of tail	Exceptions in Position Names
Rampant *erect*					Segreant for Griffin & Dragon
Salient *leaping*					Springing for Deer family
Passant *walking*					Tripping Courant *running* At Speed for Deer, Fox, Horse
Statant *standing*					
Sejant *sitting*					
Sejant Erect					
Couchant *lying*					Lodged for Deer family
Dormant *sleeping*					

Further variations of body attitudes		Further variations of head positions		Further variations of tail positions	
Combatant: (wild animals) Regarding, or Respectant: (peaceful animal)·		Guardant: (wild animal)		Extended	
Addorsed		At Gaze: (peaceful animal)		Nowed *knotted*	
				Coward *tail between legs*	
Affronte		Reguardant		Above can be further varied by a fork tail, *queue forche*	

Cadency

9th Son
8th Son
5th Son of 5th Son
7th Son
8th Son of 1
6th Son
1st Son of 5th Son
5th Son
5th Son of 3rd Son
4th Son
1st Son of 3rd Son
4th Son of 1st Son
3rd Son
1st Son of 1st Son
2nd Son
1st Son

Father's Coat of Arms

Cadency is the heraldic system of identifying an inheritance line in a coat of arms. Accordingly, marks of cadency are signs of differencing, devised to distinguish the male descendents, and later branches of a family, while perpetuating the family arms. In early heraldry this was done by modification or addition, or by introducing a new, minor charge to the existing arms. The selection and positioning of certain charges as distinct cadency marks was not standardized until the late 15th century, when a particular symbol mark was assigned to each son in their order of seniority. The heir, or first son, uses the label; second son, the *crescent;* third son, mullet; fourth son, the *martlet;* fifth son, annulet; sixth son, the *fleur de lis;* seve son, the *rose;* eighth son, the *cross mol* and the ninth son, the *double quatrefoil.* C the first nine sons have marks of cade daughters did not count — even in the Ag Chivalry.

The mark is placed in the chief of the sh unless the shield is quartered — then centered so that it extends into each of quarters. Except for the label, whic removed when the oldest son becomes head of the family, the cadency marks ca permanent. They may, however, again differenced to denote the next generat One example, shown above, is the third s first son, who incorporates a *label* ov *mullet* in his coat of arms.

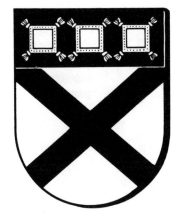

Augmentations were important charges granted by kings or governments as additions to existing coats of arms. Usually these additions were bestowed to commemorate an achievement, or a deed of great consequence. For instance, the shield of Colonel Newman, above left, was augmented by a *portcullis* because, in 1651, he successfully defended a gate that allowed Charles II to escape. The *cushion,* above center, was another charge often used as an augmentation. It represented the "carrier" on which medals, royal gifts, and official commendation scrolls were presented. The *belts,* above right, were granted as an augmentation to Sir William Pelham, who captured John of France at Poitiers in 1356. The belts are symbols of King John's sword belt. Below left, the shield is augmented by the addition of two *crowns*, probably for services rendered King and Country. And finally, Lord Nelson's arms are shown as augmented after his victories. The new and additional charges appear in chief; from a design point of view, it is clear that too much of a king's grace is not always a blessing.

Blazonry

is the special language of heraldry that depicts a shield of arms using a cant vocabulary in a prescribed sequence beginning with the surface of the shield.

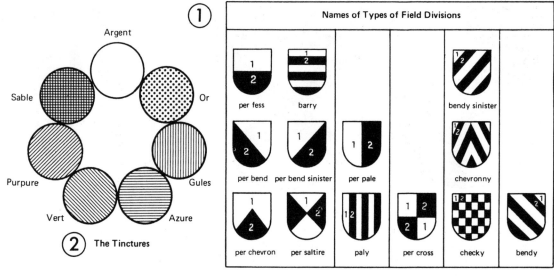

① Names of Types of Field Divisions

per fess, barry, bendy sinister, per bend, per bend sinister, per pale, chevronny, per chevron, per saltire, paly, per cross, checky, bendy

② The Tinctures

Argent, Or, Gules, Azure, Vert, Purpure, Sable

The tincture numbered 1, above, is always mentioned first. Also, if ornamental lines (e.g. indented, engrailed, etc.) partition the field, mention of the type of ornamental line precedes tincture.

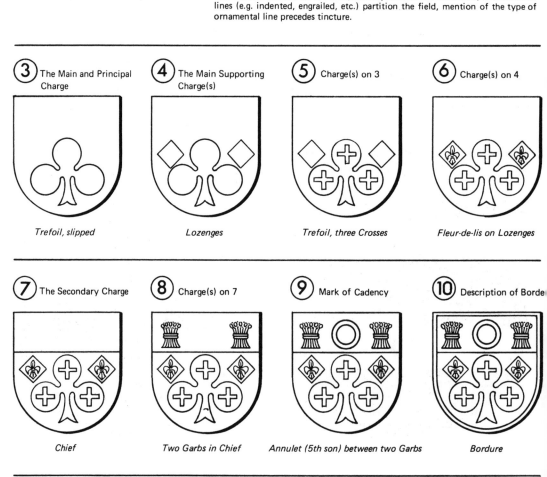

③ The Main and Principal Charge

Trefoil, slipped

④ The Main Supporting Charge(s)

Lozenges

⑤ Charge(s) on 3

Trefoil, three Crosses

⑥ Charge(s) on 4

Fleur-de-lis on Lozenges

⑦ The Secondary Charge

Chief

⑧ Charge(s) on 7

Two Garbs in Chief

⑨ Mark of Cadency

Annulet (5th son) between two Garbs

⑩ Description of Border

Bordure

A description of the crest follows; then supporters, if any. Mottoes are optional, and the mantling is usually omitted.

Blazoning, Captions, and Credits

69	Fess
70	Bar cotised
71	Bars
72	Pale
73	Pale endorsed
74	Pale parted per fess counterchanged with a pale
75	Baton couped
76	Bend
77	Pile
78	Chevron
79	Bend cotised
80	Pall
81	Chevronels
82	Bend charged with roundels
83	Counter-compony
84	Shakefork
85	Two bars gemelles with three lozenges between
86	Chevronels interlaced
87	Saltire
88	Saltire charged
89	Cross
90	Roundels in chief
91	Roundels in fess
92	Roundels in pale
93	Roundels in bend
94	Roundels in chevron
95	Bend crossed and interlaced by three bendlets sinister
96	Roundels in saltire
97	Roundels in pile
98	Parted per pale charged with roundels
99	Roundels in cross
100	Bend engrailed
101	Cross under a chief
102	Chevron and pile counterchanged
103	Bordure
104	Inescutcheon
105	Orle
106	Tressure
107	Roundels in orle
108	Lozenge
109	Fusil
110	Mascle
111	Rustre
112	Fretty
113	Label
114	Fret
115	Billet
116	Flanches
117	Gyron
118	Canton
119	Billety under a chief engrailed
120	Jerusalem cross (early form)
121	Plain cross couped
122	Patriarchal cross
123	Cross voided
124	Cross quarterly pierced fimbriated
126	Latin cross
126	Calvary cross
127	Jerusalem cross (late form)
128	Cross moline
129	Cross fourché
130	Cross cercelé
131	Cross pointed
132	Cross crosslet
133	Cross of four owls
134	Maltese cross
135	Cross floretty
136	Three lions passant in pale
137	A lion sejant affronté between two roundels in chief
138	A lion salient queue fourché over a galley
139	A lion rampant reguardant facing a crescent in chief
140	Two lion heads cojoined at body charged with fleur-de-lis
141	A lion's paw in pale erased at base charged with ermine crossed by a sword fesswise
142	A lion's paw in fess holding a sword at dexter side, under a fusil at sinister side
143	A lion statant
144	A lion sejant
145	A lion sejant erect, queue fourché
146	A lion rampant guardant
147	A lion statant reguardant over a billet

148	A lion sejant erect pierced by an arrow
149	A lion's head shot through the mouth by an arrow
150	A lion disgraced and reguardant
151	A lion's face jessant-de-lis
152	Two lion's paws erased over a bar nebuly in base
153	A lion rampant (early Gothic) over a lion's paw in dexter
154	On a fess, a lion passant under four lozenges, a lion's tail in base
155	Two lions passant in pale, quarterly counterchanged
156	A lion rampant charged with three fleurs-de-lis
157	A demi-lion over a base embattled charged with a cinquefoil
158	Per pale counterchanged two lions combatant
159	A lion statant crowned and chained over an inescutcheon charged with a castle between two crosses
160	A lion dormant with a martlet sitting on its hindquarters, over a human heart within an orle of martlets
161	Two lion's faces in pale between two flanches
162	A lion's head couped at neck
163	A crown between two lion heads combatant cojoined and couped at necks
164	A lion passant guardant (early Gothic)
165	A lion winged passant reguardant aquamenale (water-sprouting)
166	A lion passant
167	A lion rampant doubleheaded combatant and coward
168	A nag's head erased at neck
169	A horse furnished forcené over a caltrap
170	A stag lodged gorged with a crown covering a branch of oak over a chain in base
171	A fox salient over a castle
172	On a steer's head caboshed a cardinal close
173	A boar's head couped at neck
174	An elephant passant over a bar over three molets in base
175	A bear muzzled and chained to a staff raguly
176	A camel passant in front of a pyramid, a waning moon and a molet in sinister chief
177	A wolf's head, fangs exposed, couped at neck over a ducal crown
178	A wildcat on a leaved branch
179	A crown between the antlers of a deer's head caboshed
180	A ram's head caboshed under a cross cercelé
181	Two seals respectant covering a bar fesswise on an arc with three lines wavy under a row of five molets in chief
182	A kangaroo sejant, a twig of heather at sinister
183	A porcupine enraged, on a canton a spiked mace
184	Azure a stag enraged on a bar argent over a base vert charged with a fleur-de-lis, a bordure of the second charged with crosses and cinquefoils
185	Gules a buck lodged at gaze argent on a flowered meadow vert under a cross moline at sinister
186	Azure a stag courant argent over an octofoil gules
187	*Center:* or a double eagle displayed with two nag's heads addorsed sable bridled in red; an inescutcheon argent with two hammers crossed saltirewise sable; *upper left:* sable two nag's heads addorsed cojoined or, bridled in red; *upper right:* sable two nag's heads confronté or, cojoined, bridled in red, a molet in chief or; *lower left:* sable two nag's heads confronté bridled erased or, over two hammers crossed saltirewise; *lower right:* sable three nag's heads in fess couped and cojoined at neck or, bridled in red; two hammers crossed saltirewise in base or (Courtesy of Mr. H. Koplowitz)
188	An eagle preying (Courtesy of Art Director Studio News)
189	*Center:* eagle displayed inverted; *upper left:* an eagle preying; *upper right:* an eagle dismembered; *lower left:* two eagle wings a vol over a billet; *lower center:* two eagle legs erased à la cuisse; *lower right:* two eagle wing in lure over a chevron
190	*Center:* an imperial eagle displayed crowned, an inescutcheon charged with a demi vol sinister under three crowns; *below, from left to right:* an eagle close perched on a base angled between two hearts; an eagle rising wings elevated and displayed perched on base, a crown at sinister side; an eagle soaring reguardant; an eagle, wings displayed grasping a snake in its talons; an eagle soaring wings displayed inverted
191	An eagle displayed, an inescutcheon charged with a castle over three lines wavy over a ribbon mottoed
192	A demi-eagle
193	An eagle perched close
194	An eagle close perched on a sword with an olive branch
195	An eagle displayed
196	*Left:* an eagle displayed; *right:* an eagle displayed inverted
197	Alerion
198	Alerion
199	*Left:* a martlet; *below, left to top right:* a martlet without legs, without feet, with legs and feet; with legs and feet (old version), with legs and feet (new version)
200	A dove diving between two latin crosses
201	Two swallows flying fesswise
202	A swan on two bars wavy, moon in plenitude in dexter chief
203	An owl affronté
204	Two ravens close perched on a bar
205	A falcon belled covering a fess
206	A peacock in its pride
207	A rooster perched on a base per chevron
208	An ostrich running with a broken chain under a sun in its glory
209	Azure a pelican in its piety argent, a sun or in chief sinister
210	An escallop between three roundels
211	Three fishes hauriant
212	A dolphin embowed

213	Three fishes naiant
214	A mermaid with mirror and comb
215	A sealion covered by a bar wavy in fess, a molet in sinister chief
216	A fish diving bend sinisterwise into a net bendwise
217	A sailfish embowed
218	A barbel's head hauriant between two whelk shells in chief
219	A salamander
220	Or a dolphin proper embowed over a base wavy azure
221	A dragon segreant argent
222	Sable a tyger rampant argent
223	Sable a pegasus rising over a molet argent
224	Sable a unicorn bearded in red argent
225	Sable a griffin segreant argent
226	Sable an opinicus sejant argent
227	Or a cockatrice sejant proper
228	A wyvern rampant
229	A male griffin sejant sable spiked and horned in azure
230	Sable azure per pale a griffin sejant holding a trademark of a printing ink factory (Courtesy of Jaenecke-Schneemann, Hannover, Germany)
231	An opinicus sejant
232	Moon in plenitude (or, in her complement)
233	Moon in her crescent
234	Sunburst
235	Estoiles
236	A white rose en soleil
237	Molet
238	Planta genista
239	Dogwood slipped and fructed
240	Moon in her increscent
241	Moon in her decrescent
242	Argent a thunderbolt twisted in sable and azure (or gules) wings on both sides sable, striking palewise from clouds in chief between four jagged darts of lightning saltirewise azure
243	Sun in his glory (or, in his splendor)
244	A tree eradicated and fructed
245	An octofoil
246	A trefoil between two billets in chief
247	Three oakleaves between two acorns in chief
248	A thistle
249	A winestock with two bunches of grapes
250	A garb in a garland
251	A cross in a crown of thorns
252	A rose slipped and leaved
253	Fleur-de-lis
254	Azure a bell with a pull argent
255	Azure an anchor between two flags
256	Azure a harness with seven hawk bells argent
257	Azure a two-arched bridge argent
258	Azure a galley between two inescutcheons argent, sail adorned with a cross moline between four plain crosses
259	Azure a quill in pale covering a book open under three crowns argent
260	Azure a wagon wheel over a bar dancetty argent
261	Sable three belt buckles palewise under a row of three martlets in chief argent
262	Sable a Schellenbaum with a lion argent on top
263	Sable a castle over a rose in base argent a label
264	A portcullis with chains
265	Sable two keys saltirewise between two billets in chief and base argent
266	Azure a head of a halberd in pale covering a lion passant argent
267	Azure two arrows saltirewise between four roundels argent
268	Azure a sword in pale covered by a crown at fesspoint argent
269	Azure a crossbow in pale between two arrows argent
270	Azure three caltraps over a chevron abaissé
271	Azure a chess knight over a fetterlock in base argent
272 273 274	Different renditions of a clarion
275 276 277	Variations of the millrind
278	A carbuncle
279	A water bouget
280	A manche
281	Azure gules per pale counterchanged throughout an eagle displayed or (used as tapestry)
282	Gules an eagle displayed inverted, on wingtips two eagle heads combating each other argent; embattled or (Early Gothic, about 1300). Gules azure parted by a bend sinister or; between two eagle heads erased combating each other argent (Gothic, about 1350). Gules an eagle displayed inverted argent embattled or; an inescutcheon or charged with a human heart gules (Late Gothic, about 1450). Gules a demi-eagle wings displayed inverted argent over a chevron or; on a base azure a demi-lion or; on an inescutcheon or a human heart gules; a bordure or (Early Renaissance, about 1500). Gules azure impaled an eagle displayed inverted argent; an inescutcheon or with a human heart gules; a lion rampant or, a bordure or (Late Renaissance, about 1650). Gules azure divided by a bar or a demi-eagle displayed inverted argent;

an inescutcheon or with a human heart gules; a lion passant or, a bordure or (Baroque, about 1700). Gules azure divided by a bar or, a demi-eagle displayed inverted argent; a chevron gules over a base sable with a bunch of grapes or (Rococo, about 1750). Azure gules per pale an eagle displayed inverted argent issuant from a base per chevron sable with a bunch of grapes or; two inescutcheons on wingtips or with a vineleaf vert (20th Century)

283   Sable a cross moline between four roundels or, an inescutcheon gules with a cinquefoil or

284   Azure gules per pale a lion sejant, enraged and coward or, collared and held by a chain argent to the sinister side under a crown or

285   Within a garter with a crown; gules a phoenix displayed rising from flames or

286   A tree trunk raguly couped at top and bottom, three oak leaves on both sides sprouting out

287   The personal arms of Dr. C. Bartlett: Azure a pear tree fructed proper growing on a mound of grass vert; an inescutcheon argent, five pallets gules under a chief azure with three molets argent (Courtesy of Dr. C. Bartlett, Boston)

288   The personal arms of Mr. P. Fishel: Azure a fish hauriant palewise between three and three fishes flanchwise and two roundels in chief argent (Courtesy of Mr. P. Fishel, New York)

289   The personal arms of Mr. J. Swanson: Gules a swan carrying a little swan on his back, on a base wavy argent (Courtesy of Mr. J. Swanson, Chicago)

290   A label design for bottled cocktails: Gules a rooster (cock) reguardant argent (Courtesy of Heublein, Inc., Hartford, Conn.)

291   The personal arms of Mr. H. Dudley: Gules a lion rampant or (Courtesy of Mr. H. Dudley, Washington, D.C.)

292   The personal arms of Dr. O. Schwarz: Sable three inescutcheons with three chevronels counterchanged palewise sable argent in a bordure argent (Courtesy of Dr. O. Schwarz, New York)

293   A rebus proposed for Prof. Dr. H. G. Hillebrecht, Hannover, Germany, (depicting his name): Argent four hemp plants slipped, seeded and rooted proper behind a hemp-bracket sable

294   A proposed personal arms for Prof. H. G. Hillebrecht, Hannover, Germany (commemorating a career triumph): Gules three towers issuant from a bar embattled covering two spades between the towers, blades going down to base argent

295⎫
296⎬   Combs for combing flax
297⎭   Author's personal arms (old version): Or three bleeding hearts gules slipped and leaved vert issuant from a bar dancetty sable

298   Author's personal arms (revised): Argent a tree trunk raguly sable with two human hearts sprouting out on both sides charged with two castles over a bar dancetty, overall azure

299   An example of an unusual personal arms: Gules a wyvern curled, enraged and dismembered argent

300   A bookplate belonging to George Washington: Argent two bars under three molets fesswise in chief gules

301   An ex libris: Vert an elk antler curved around a billet charged with a sword in dexter argent (Courtesy of Miss Dora Deves, Hannover, Germany)

302   An ex libris: Vert two octofoils slipped and leaved palewise or (Courtesy of Mr. Robert R. Maller, Long Island)

303   An ex libris: Azure a rooster as a weathervane perched on an arrow fesswise on top of two chevronels in base argent (Courtesy of Miss Karin Hahn, Hannover, Germany)

304   An ex libris: Vert a quill in a lyre between two towers of a castle on a base wavy argent; three weights in a base sable (Courtesy of Mr. Matthew P. Murgio, New York)

305⎫
306⎬   Renditions of the American seal
307⎭   Arms of the City of Hannover: Gules a castle argent with a lion statant or between its towers; an inescutcheon or with trefoil vert in the open door in base (Courtesy of the City of Hannover, Germany)

308   Arms for a small Mediterranean fishing village: Three fishes hauriant in pale between six plain crosses at dexter and sinister one in base

309   Coat of arms of the late Cardinal Spellman

310   A redesign of Cardinal Spellman's coat of arms

311   Seal of the Bishop of Louisiana: A pelican in her piety; a chief charged with a molet and a plough

312   A guild symbol: A square between three dividers 2:1 (Carpenters' Hall, Philadelphia)

313   An illustration used in a promotional brochure of a commercial printing house: Vert three printing rollers fesswise in pale between two printing pads in chief and base. (Courtesy of Gebr. Jaenecke, Hannover, Germany)

314   A school insignia: Argent the bristles of a paint brush between two six-leaved trees on a base; one small tree in dexter one in sinister vert

315   A necklabel for a whiskey bottle: Three lions passant guardant in pale

316   A centerpiece for a vodka label adapted from the Tsar's emblem: An imperial eagle crowned and ribboned; an inescutcheon with St. George killing the dragon (Courtesy of Heublein Inc., Hartford, Conn.)

317   A trademark for a leather manufacturer: A lizard crowned (Courtesy of Deitsch Bros., New York)

318   A label centerpiece design for a brewery

319   A colophon for a technical book publisher

320   A trademark (Courtesy of Koudelka Photomounts, New York)

321   A design for an aircraft manufacturer

322   A promotional piece designed for a marketing firm (Courtesy of Tietgen Research Associates, New York)

323   A book jacket design

324   A trademark design for a radio station

325   A playing card design for Arcis Plastic Playing Cards, New York.

326   Package or design for printing inks: Imperator in full regalia (Courtesy of Jaenecke-Schneemann, Hannover, Germany)

327   Trademark for a button manufacturer

328   The personal arms of Mr. Henry Rosenberg: Argent gules per chevron three red roses 1:2, in chevron three roses 1:2 argent (Courtesy of Mr. Henry Rosenberg, New York)

329   The great arms of the City of Hannover, Germany

329

GLOSSARY-INDEX